D1140813

Books should be returned on or before the
last date stamped below.

11. JUN. 1979

NORTH EAST of SCOTLAND LIBRARY SERVICE
14 Crown Terrace, Aberdeen

FRASERBURGH

BIRNBAUM, Hubert C.

PSL guide to cameras

1. 771.3

PSL Guide to
Cameras

PSL Guide to

Cameras

Hubert C. Birnbaum

Patrick Stephens Ltd.
Cambridge, England

Note: In the appendix of this book, you will find a table for converting measurements to the metric system. You will also find a table for ASA and DIN equivalents.

771.3
1

Copyright ©1978 by Hubert C. Birnbaum.

All rights reserved. No part of this book may be reproduced in any form whatsoever without written permission from the publisher.

Published in Great Britain by Patrick Stephens Limited

British Library Cataloguing in Publication Data
Birnbaum, Hubert C.
PSL guide to cameras.—(PSL photo guides).
1. Cameras—Amateurs' manuals
I. Title
770'.282 TR250

ISBN 085059 369 7 (softbound)
ISBN 085059 368 9 (hardbound)

Manufactured in the United States of America

To my mother, Adele Hugel Birnbaum, with love.

Contents

1

Introduction

Choosing a camera was much easier in the earliest days of photography than it is today, although photography itself was far more difficult. Once you knew what you wanted the camera to do, you looked over a relatively limited variety of brands and types, most of which did the same things in virtually the same way. If your needs couldn't be filled off the shelf, and a fairly small shelf at that, your next step would be to have a skilled craftsman make you the camera of your dreams, and you might even commission an optical expert to design and construct a lens to your specifications. Much thought and effort were required on the part of all parties to the transaction, but the basic possibilities were quite limited.

Today, the would-be camera buyer risks complete befuddlement by the assortment of photographic equipment to be found in the average neighborhood camera shop, let alone the dazzling array of cameras available at major photo dealers. From the serviceable but Spartan low-cost snapshot camera to the exquisitely made, high-technology electronic marvels that cost as much as a subcompact car, the variety of types, sizes, brands, and models boggles the mind. And the choice becomes even more difficult if you are willing to consider discontinued models, new or used, that are still perfectly good picture-making machines, although lacking the latest tailfins.

This technological proliferation is, of course, a source of joy to well-informed professional and advanced amateur photographers. A wide variety of specialized photographic needs can now be met with off-the-shelf cameras and accessories. For most

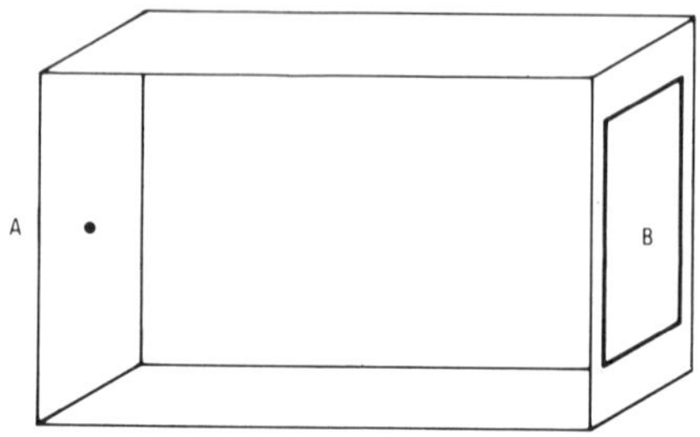

In its simplest form, a camera is merely a lighttight box with an image-forming pinhole or lens (A) at one end and a piece of film (B) held at the other.

photographers, most of the time, it is simply not necessary to incur the expense of custom-madc photographic equipment for any but the most esoteric applications.

The other side of the coin, though, is that picking the "right" camera can appear to be a nearly insurmountable problem to the person who hasn't devoted a good deal of time reading photographic literature. Of the hundreds of cameras of various shapes and sizes gleaming in the dealer's showcases, which one will be the best choice? This book is designed to help you answer that question for yourself.

The following chapters explore various basic features, functions, and characteristics that distinguish one camera type from another, and relate them to actual photographic circumstances and the way cameras are used. Later chapters discuss specific camera types both in terms of the basic "building-block" characteristics, and the practical advantages and disadvantages they offer when combined.

Although modern cameras may appear to be terribly complex at first glance, and in fact can contain hundreds of tiny parts interacting in intricate ways, they are not at all hard to understand from a functional standpoint. Fortunately, it is the functional standpoint that is most important to the photographer. By examining the various components of cameras from a pragmatic, functional point of view, then matching them against your particular set of photographic needs, you can come up with an accurate profile of the features that will serve you best.

Even if you cannot find in any one camera type a composite of all the features you need or want, you will probably find most of them embodied in at least one type of camera. Realistically, you may find that you have to make a few compromises or trade-offs, giving up one feature you want to get another that you want a bit more. Or you may conclude that no one camera type can cover all your needs, but two different types will coexist in your photographic life very happily, indeed. And as you tally various features, functions, and characteristics against your list of photographic requirements, you may be pleased to discover that you can do without quite a few of the elaborate features that your photographer friends find indispensable.

The key to putting the information in this book to work for you lies in your willingness to appraise your photographic requirements as objectively as possible. This may not be as easy as it sounds. A great deal of camera advertising, associated commercial literature, and many articles in the amateur photographic press imply that "professional" means good and anything other than professional is less good. Accordingly, if you've had a recent overdose of such material, you may find yourself confusing your needs with those of a fashion photographer whose work is currently in vogue, or a well-known sports photographer who became famous covering the winter Olympics, or some other photographic folk hero. While it is a blessing to the photographic industry that tens of thousands of people buy elaborate cameras each year with the secret hope that they will become rich, famous photographers by buying the same kinds of cameras used by the current crop of rich, famous photographers, it is not always an undiluted blessing for the purchasers. Unless you plan to make the same kinds of pictures under the same conditions the professional encounters, you may end up putting yourself at a considerable photographic and financial disadvantage by equipping yourself similarly.

As a starting point, then, draw up a list of the types of pictures you wish to make. Consider the kinds of photos you've enjoyed making in the recent past, if you're already a camera owner; add to the list categories of photographs you would like to make but may not have been able to because of equipment limitations. Honesty with yourself is essential in compiling this list, because it will be the basis for some hardheaded decision-making later.

When you've completed the list, review it skeptically with regard to types of photos you would like to make but couldn't because of the equipment you were using. Ask yourself in each case if the pictures were not made because the available equipment really couldn't handle the situation or if you were actually not sufficiently motivated to find the means or the time. Even

Almost any fast-handling, easy-to-use camera can do a good job recording fleeting personal moments.

fairly simple cameras can often be adapted or accessorized to make certain types of pictures that are not immediately associated with them. For example, many different camera types can be adapted easily to make pictures through a microscope. If you've listed photographs through a microscope as a type you wish to make, but have never actually determined whether or not your current camera could be adapted to making them, you would be well advised not to place undue emphasis on suitability for photomicrography as a criterion for selecting your next camera. In any case, if you've been reasonably candid in compiling your list, it will give you an accurate overview of how you actually use a camera and how you wish to use one. You will be well prepared to answer the question, "What do you want a camera to do for you?" and to ask in turn, "Can this camera make the following specific types of pictures easily and well?"

Another personal factor to consider carefully in selecting a camera that will be best for you is your degree of involvement with photography. Is photography something you endure because there's no other way for you to get pictures of people, places, and things that interest you? Are you a photographic hobbyist who finds pleasure in the creative and technical challenges of photography? Or are you so passionately involved with photography that you see it as the dominant force in your life? There is neither shame nor virtue in any position on the scale of photographic involvement that runs from none to total, but it does pay off handsomely in selecting equipment sensibly to know where you stand, and to admit it.

Incidentally, some courage may be needed in this regard to resist peer-group pressure. Friends or family who are photographic equipment enthusiasts will be almost certain to look askance at a simple snapshot camera, even if it is precisely what you need for documenting vacations and family events. Conversely, other people who know and love you may openly question your sanity for investing in high-quality, versatile equipment you really need to work on a serious project.

Once you've examined the pattern of your picture-taking, current and proposed, and confessed your involvement or lack of it in the photographic process, you will have a very clear notion of who you are as a photographer. In the following chapters, you will see what various components of a camera do, how they are combined in different types of cameras, and how individual components and various combinations of them help or hinder in various photographic applications. By evaluating the various features and characteristics of different camera types in terms of your personal preferences and needs, you will be able to determine which camera type or types will serve you best, both now and in the foreseeable future.

One aspect of selecting a camera is, unfortunately, beyond the scope of this book. Because of the long lead time involved in preparing a book manuscript and the rapid changes that occur in the photographic equipment market with regard to specific camera brands and models within a brand, specific brands and models cannot be recommended as ultimate answers to various photographic problems. To be sure, references to and illustrations of specific cameras and accessories do occur on the following pages. In most cases the item is shown or discussed as an example of its type to help clarify a relevant point. Because a particular brand or model is mentioned or shown should not, however, be construed as an endorsement.

As we begin to explore the many characteristics and features that are combined in various ways to create different types of cameras, it may be comforting to keep in mind the following great truth: A camera is simply a lighttight box with a hole for admitting image-forming light at one end and a means for holding a piece of film at the other. All else is embellishment.

2

Film Types, Sizes, and Formats

Conventional photography does not exist without film on which to record the image formed by the camera lens. The type of film, its size, physical characteristics, and image-forming characteristics profoundly affect the appearance of the final image and the configuration of the cameras in which the film is used.

General-purpose photographic films fall into two main categories: negative and positive. *Negative* film records the image in reversed tones, with light subject areas represented by dark tones on film and dark subject areas rendered as relatively light or clear portions on the negative. The tonally reversed film negative is used to print a same-sized or enlarged positive print or transparency in which tonal values correspond approximately to those of the original subject. Negative films are available in both black-and-white and color emulsions.

Positive film produces a tonally correct rendition of the subject directly on the piece of film in the camera, which becomes the final picture. Most commonly used positive films are color films intended for projection and/or photomechanical reproduction on the printed page. (They may also be used to produce color prints.) The finished, processed original is referred to as a transparency. Small transparencies suitable for projection are often popularly called slides. Positive films are also known as reversal films, because during processing, a negative image that is initially developed is further processed, or reversed, to form the final positive image.

FILM SPEED

Both positive and negative films may be further categorized in terms of their sensitivity to light, which is commonly referred to as film speed. In the United States, film speed is expressed numerically by ASA (American Standards Association)* numbers. The higher a film's ASA speed, the greater its sensitivity to light. Relative film speeds are easy to determine by comparing the respective ASA numbers. Each time the ASA speed doubles, the amount of light required to produce a given level of exposure is halved. A film rated at ASA 50, for example, is twice as fast as one rated at ASA 25, and half as fast as one rated at ASA 100.

High-speed films, also called *fast films*, with ASA speeds of 400 or over, are useful for photographing in subdued light, or in bright light when fast shutter speeds are required to freeze action. *Low-speed*, or *slow films*, with ASA speeds of 25 to 32, are often used despite their slowness because their image-forming characteristics are sometimes more desirable than those of high-speed films. As a rule, slow-speed films tend to produce somewhat sharper, finer-grained, higher-contrast, and more sparkling images than high-speed films. Medium-speed films, as the designation implies, are middle-of-the-road materials in terms of speed and other attributes. Their ASA speeds range from about 50 to 200.

A slow, fine-grain film with characteristically high sharpness and inherent contrast produced dramatic rendition of power plant. Resolution recorded fine detail, contrast separated it, and acutance delineated edged clearly.

* The letters ASA stand for American Standards Association, which has long since changed its name to American National Standards Institute (ANSI). The ASA designation continues to be used with film-speed ratings determined according to ANSI standards. ASA to DIN conversion can be found in the appendix.

An extremely high-speed, grainy film with low contrast and mediocre sharpness produced a soft, gentle print of peaceful park scene.

OTHER CHARACTERISTICS

Although most film is chosen purely by deciding on color vs. black-and-white, prints vs. slides, and possibly a speed range matched to expected light intensity or action-stopping requirements, there are additional film characteristics to be considered if you wish to control the appearance of the final image.

Edge sharpness, or *acutance,* is the ability of the film to produce a clean, sharp boundary between clearly defined adjacent areas of different tones. For example, in a close-up photograph of a bright razor's edge against a contrasting background, a high-acutance film should ideally produce a razor-edge demarcation along the razor's edge.

Resolution is the film's ability to record very fine detail clearly. In the hypothetical photograph of the razor's edge, resolution more than acutance would allow you to see the faint tool marks that polishing failed to remove from the steel.

Graininess in a film manifests itself as a gritty, granular texture when the film is viewed under high magnification or is used to make a considerably enlarged print or projection.

Contrast relates to a film's ability to record brightness differences in the subject. A moderate-contrast film will record light, dark, and in-between subject brightnesses plausibly with respect to each other and to the overall appearance of the subject. High-contrast films tend to exaggerate the contrast of light and shadow in the original scene, often producing a harsh, soot-and-whitewash effect when the original subject is itself high in contrast. Low-contrast films tend to reduce contrast, and may produce somewhat flat-looking results when the original scene is low in contrast.

Traditionally, low-speed films tend to exhibit excellent edge sharpness and resolution, low graininess, and moderate to high contrast. High-speed films have been associated with lower acutance and resolution, more noticeable graininess, and moderate to low contrast. While these rules of thumb are still generally valid, as films improve, it becomes increasingly difficult to force them into this convenient set of patterns. Happy anomalies are occurring, such as low-speed films with very manageable contrast, and high-speed films with excellent edge sharpness and resolution, and low graininess.

It should be noted that edge sharpness, resolution, graininess, and contrast are essentially neutral characteristics. They become good or bad in specific applications. For example, although high acutance and resolution, low graininess, and moderate to high contrast might form an ideal combination for the architectural photographer, it could be sheer poison for a portrait photographer about to photograph a middle-aged woman. Conversely, a "softer" film that is ideal for photographing middle-aged portrait subjects might be a very poor choice for architecture.

Nonetheless, it is also true that a photographer can reduce effective film sharpness, increase apparent graininess, and alter contrast characteristics through various exposure and processing manipulations, but there is absolutely nothing he can do to make an inherently unsharp, grainy film produce a very sharp, grainless picture. Therefore, for most purposes it is reasonable to assume that high sharpness and resolution, low graininess, and moderate contrast represent desirable characteristics.

Additional film characteristics peculiar to color materials include color balance and color rendition.

Color balance is a gross bias in color sensitivity, built in at the factory, that permits a type of film to record colors plausibly when exposed under a specific type of illumination. Typically, color films are balanced for compatibility with daylight and electronic flash, or for studio-type tungsten lighting.

Color rendition is a somewhat more subtle dimension of color films, and highly subjective. It refers to a given film's propensity for rendering colors in a characteristic way. If you photograph the same person or color chart with six different color films under identical conditions, you are likely to end up looking at six perceptibly different versions of the test scene. None is likely to be a literally correct color reproduction of the original scene. All should be fairly believable, and one or more will probably strike you as more pleasing than the others, depending on your personal preferences and preconceptions about how the subject *should* look, regardless of how it *does* look.

All of the preceding film characteristics influence the appearance of the final picture. However, even more important in creating the final visual impression is the simple fact of film size.

FILM SIZE

The size of the piece of film exposed in the camera affects the appearance of the finished picture in two ways: 1) it limits the minimum size of the camera in which it is exposed; and 2) it limits the maximum size of the final picture as viewed that will retain adequate image quality. Both points are worth exploring.

From most photographers' standpoints, a small, light camera, with small, light accessories, provides great freedom of movement and permits easily making very spontaneous pictures. Particularly, for the amateur, more convenient equipment means greater likelihood that it will be used, and fewer reservations about being seriously encumbered while not actually taking pictures. Obviously, the ideal camera would be very small, very light, and capable of handling all photographic tasks. The catch is that small cameras accept only small pieces of film, which can do many jobs well but cannot do all jobs with the degree of technical quality that may be required. The problem consists of two unhappily related factors: The final image as viewed is nearly always enlarged relative to the original image recorded in the camera; and enlargement magnifies imperfections along with the detail that forms the picture.

The more the camera original is magnified to produce the final picture, the less sharp it looks and the more grainy it appears. The less the original is magnified, the better it will retain sharpness and the less it will reveal the inherent graininess of the film. This is why films and cameras are available in a great variety of sizes.

As a basic principle, it is safe to assume that, all other factors being equal, a good big piece of film will always beat a good small piece of film of the same type. The big piece of film provides more area on which to record the detail in the scene, and then requires less magnification to produce a given size of final picture.

Having explored inherent film characteristics, let's look at a variety of film sizes and "packagings." All are in current production as this is being written. (Not all formats in production will be covered, because some are not suitable for general-purpose photography, and others have not achieved sufficient popularity to represent more than a cult symbol.)

110 CARTRIDGE FILM

The 110 film cartridge is designed primarily for amateur snapshot use, and produces the smallest original transparency or negative of any popular film size: 13 × 17 mm. The plastic cartridge provides for literally foolproof drop-in film loading without threading or need to touch the film itself in any way. No rewinding of film is necessary after the last exposure has been made. And the cartridge is notched according to a standardized system to key a camera's exposure system to the sensitivity of the film in the cartridge. The actual strip of film, coiled in a film chamber on the right side of the cartridge, is transported across a rigid "bridge" that forms the film channel and pressure plate, and accumulates on a take-up spool in a chamber on the left side of the cartridge. The film is backed by an opaque paper strip, as is used with larger roll-film sizes, that carries printed frame numbers visible through a viewing port in the cartridge back. Cartridges contain enough film for 12 or 20 exposures, depending on film type.

Because 110 film is considered an amateur format, the selection of films in 110 cartridges is limited to a few general-purpose types from each major manufacturer. This is probably because of the correct assumption by manufacturers that most users neither need nor want a vast choice of exotic films to record

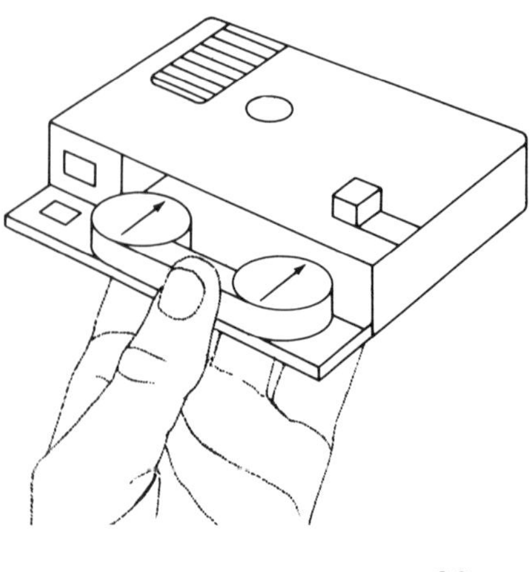

Cartridge-loading 110 (shown) and 126 films offer exceptionally easy drop-in camera loading.

family events and vacation scenes under generally favorable lighting conditions. Only a few high-speed films are available in 110 size because the great degree of enlargement required with a tiny original image tends to degrade photographic quality quickly as film graininess becomes more pronounced.

The key charm of 110 film, aside from its ease of use, is the small size of the cartridge, which permits very small, compact cameras to be designed for it. Although even smaller film cartridges were produced prior to the introduction of 110 by Eastman Kodak Company, none of the earlier miniformats had the advantage of factory-packed Kodak film and high-quality Kodak photofinishing. Thus, such subminiatures as the Minox remained specialty cameras for a relatively small coterie of enthusiasts. Kodak, in contrast, brought to the public a coordinated package of small, harmonica-shaped Pocket Instamatic cameras, 110 film, and appropriate processing services, along with a line of small slide projectors for 110 transparencies.

Consistent with the amateur orientation of the 110 format, the cameras designed for it are primarily point-and-shoot snapshot types that stress ease of operation. Nonetheless, many are capable of producing sharp, fine-quality images that hold up surprisingly well under even unreasonable degrees of enlargement. Thus, better-quality 110 cartridge cameras have found favor not only as main cameras for snapshooters but also as second cameras for photo hobbyists and serious photographers.

126 CARTRIDGE FILM

The 126 film format is the obsolescent predecessor of the 110 size. The 126 film cartridge is similar to the 110 cartridge, but larger, and the film frame is 28 × 28 mm. As with 110, 126 film is available in lengths of 12 or 20 exposures, according to film type. The chief virtues of 126 film are drop-in loading simplicity and automatic film-speed setting via a cartridge notching system similar to that used later for 110 film cartridges. The 126 film cartridge and film frame are not small enough to permit much in the way of camera miniaturization, and consequently, most 126 cameras are not dramatically smaller than popular compact 35 mm snapshot cameras. Few film types are available in 126 cartridges, and currently, few 126 cartridge cameras are being produced. Some older models may still be available new from existing inventories, and many are available on the used market.

The only advantage 126 has over 110 is the larger film frame, which requires less enlarging to make a print of a given size. Since snapshots are seldom enlarged beyond roughly post-card size, this advantage is more theoretical than practical.

35 mm FILM

For professional and amateur photographers alike, 35 mm is by far the most popular film size, and this is reflected in the vast variety of 35 mm films available. Besides the usual assortment of color negative, color positive, and black-and-white negative films spanning the speed spectrum from very slow to extremely fast, many special-purpose emulsions with esoteric applications are available to the 35 mm photographer. And as might be expected, an incredible variety of cameras is on the market in 35 mm size, ranging from very simple snapshot cameras to high-technology photographic systems that encompass enough accessories to cope with nearly any subject or situation.

As supplied, ready for loading into a 35 mm camera, 35 mm film is contained in a lighttight metal or plastic magazine, sometimes called a cartridge or cassette. The film is wound on a spool inside the magazine, and the film end is secured to the spool, usually with tape or a small clamp or prong. The film leader protrudes from the magazine through lighttight feed lips lined with a soft, dark light-baffling material. Standard film lengths provide 20, 24, or 36 full-frame exposures measuring 24 × 36 mm (outside the U.S., 12-exposure magazines are sometimes encountered as well). A few "half-frame" 35 mm cameras make twice as many exposures per roll, with an image frame measuring only 18 × 24 mm. No paper backing is used. A row of evenly

Perforated 35 mm film in magazines and long bulk rolls offers great variety of film types. Cameras that use it range from simple snapshot models to elaborate professional system cameras. Wider-gauge 70 mm edge-perforated film is used in special-purpose professional cameras.

Among special-purpose films available in 35 mm magazines, a black-and-white infrared-sensitive emulsion produced this eerie cityscape.

spaced sprocket holes runs along each edge of the film strip, providing positive film advance by toothed sprocket-drive wheels in the camera body.

The 35 mm film strip comes by its strong resemblance to motion picture film because it *was* movie film in the beginning. Only after the Leica camera was introduced in 1925 did "35 mm" begin prominently to be identified with still photography.

Because the 35 mm film magazine consists of only one film chamber, conventional 35 mm cameras require both a film-advance and a film-rewind system. After the roll of unbacked film is exposed and wound on the camera's integral take-up spool, the film must be rewound into the magazine from which it fed before the camera back is opened and the film removed from the camera. The chief advantage of the system is that a long length of film is contained in a small magazine, saving space and relieving the photographer of the necessity of reloading the camera frequently. A concomitant drawback is that the film has to make an additional pass through the camera as it is rewound into its magazine, doubling the opportunity for it to be scratched or abraded. In practice, this drawback has proven more theoretical than real.

High-speed black-and-white 35 mm film captured fatigue of late Adlai Stevenson under subdued lighting in United Nations General Assembly Hall.

In addition to factory-loaded magazines, 35 mm film is available in long rolls for darkroom loading into empty magazines. Lengths range from 27½ feet to several hundred feet, depending upon film type and manufacturer. A photographer may choose to load magazines by hand with bulk film to reduce costs, to obtain odd-length loads for particular applications, or because a special-purpose film desired is simply not available in factory-loaded magazines. Another reason for "rolling your own" may be to take advantage of the opportunity to use special high-precision film magazines available for several high-quality cameras. These camera-brand film magazines, which tend to be costly, use rotating inner and outer shells to protect the film from light instead of padded feed lips, which rub against the delicate film surfaces during the advance and rewind motions. Similarly constructed, over-size cartridges holding lengths of film sufficient for up to 250 or more exposures are also on the market for use with accessory bulk-magazine film backs for several 35 mm "system" cameras. They permit extended shooting sessions without need for frequent interruptions to reload.

Opponents of bulk loading cite the risks of getting dirt and scratches on the film while handling it in the dark, and contend that film manufacturers are more consistent and expert at loading magazines than the individual photographer is likely to be. In practical terms, for most photographers factory-loaded magazines are more desirable.

In its inception, one of the advantages the small 35 mm film frame provided was the opportunity to make small, lightweight cameras that could hold enough film at one loading to more than cover the average photographer's immediate needs. This advantage is as real today as it was in the early days of 35 mm photography. It allows a photographer to equip himself or herself fully without assuming an intolerable burden of equipment and extra film. The small camera allows great freedom of movement and permits the photographer to work inconspicuously in candid or spontaneous situations. And most 35 mm cameras can be operated rapidly, with or without accessory electric motor drives or film winders. Coupled with their large film capacity, this speedy operating capability suits them well to recording rapidly changing situations such as sports events and news happenings. Clearly, 35 mm is also suitable for capturing the fleeting events of daily life.

With all these advantages, one may wonder why the 35 mm format has not eliminated the need for larger formats. The answer brings us full circle to the question of size. The same film improvements that made big blow-ups from small negatives an attractive reality have made bigger blow-ups from bigger negatives an equally attractive reality for many photographers and end users of photography. Furthermore, the small size that makes 35 mm cameras and accessories so appealing, also prevents them from incorporating certain features that can be built into larger cameras. As an all-around, general-purpose, workhorse format, though, it would be hard to find a more versatile, adaptable film/camera combination than 35 mm.

120 ROLL FILM

Once an extremely popular film size among amateur photographers, 120 roll film is now used largely by professionals. This shift in popularity is the result of several forces acting more or less simultaneously. The developments in film, processing, and photographic equipment that made 35 mm and smaller formats feasible for amateur use by improving final picture quality have also benefited the professional photographer. Consequently, many professional assignments are shot on smaller film sizes than in the past, including 35 mm. However, for many professional applications, the 35 mm frame is too small from the standpoints of enlargeability, retouching, reproduction quality, and easy editing by the client. The 120 roll-film size, then, bridges the gap between the too-small 35 mm on one side and what is often a too-large sheet-film size on the other.

Physically, a roll of 120 film consists of a length of photographic film taped at its leading end to a long strip of opaque backing paper. The film and backing paper are wound around a slender flanged spool. The extra lengths of backing paper at each end of the film roll protect the film from light during camera loading and unloading. The film spool flanges prevent light from striking the edges of the film. The core of the film spool is slotted to accept a short tab of backing paper, which keeps the film-and-paper coil from slipping around the core, yet permits it to easily pull free after the roll has been wound off the supply spool. The backing paper's outer side is imprinted with appropriately spaced frame numbers and a variety of start marks suitable for different types of cameras and film magazines.

Cameras designed for 120 roll film may have an integral film chamber accepting a full roll on the feed side of the film gate and an empty spool on the take-up side; an integral film chamber that accepts an insert carrying both the full roll and a take-up spool, which may be dropped into place in the camera as a unit; or a completely interchangeable film magazine containing the loaded roll and take-up spool. Interchangeable magazines are usually equipped with a removable dark slide to cover the film gate, thus allowing magazines to be changed in mid-roll without light striking the film in the aperture.

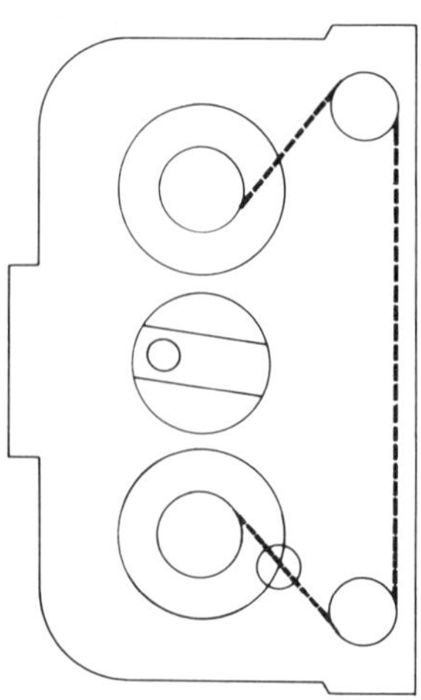

In interchangeable film magazine for 6 X 6 cm SLR camera, paper-backed 120 film (dashed line) feeds from full spool (bottom) past film gate and onto take-up spool (top).

Regardless of the particular design, loading involves placing a full 120 roll on the feed side of the film system, engaging the paper leader tab in the slot of the take-up spool, and winding off paper backing with the camera or magazine back closed until film is in position in the film gate of the camera or film magazine. Initial positioning of the first frame may be done automatically or semi-automatically by the camera itself, via a sensing mechanism that "feels" the greater thickness where the film begins, or visually, by looking through a viewing port in the magazine or camera back to spot the appropriate frame number or index mark printed on the backing paper.

Advancing the film is done by a mechanism that turns the take-up spool enough to drag the appropriate length of film and backing paper from the feed spool while winding exposed film with its backing onto the take-up spool. At the end of the roll, the film transport is operated until all exposed film and its backing are wound onto the take-up spool. The magazine or camera is opened, the end of the roll is sealed closed with a strip of gummed tape pre-fastened at one end to the backing, and the roll is removed from the take-up chamber for processing. The empty feed spool is moved to the take-up chamber, where it will serve as the take-up spool for the next roll of film.

Advantages of this system are that the film makes only a single trip through the camera and is protected fully on one side by its backing paper, thus reducing the likelihood of scratches and abrasion from contact with the camera interior or dirt and grit that may have infiltrated the body. Each roll of film is comparatively compact and lightweight, given the size of the film frame (which we'll discuss shortly), although much less so than 35 mm film.

Disadvantages of the system include awkwardness in loading and unloading because of the need to unseal and seal rolls carefully and to juggle spools from chamber to chamber, and the possibility of feeding problems for a variety of reasons ranging from the leader tab's slipping out of the slot in the take-up spool, to skewed winding on the take-up spool from careless alignment of the backing paper edges with the spool flanges. These are problems that normally diminish as the user's familiarity with the system increases. A harder problem to deal with is occasional unsharpness in a picture that was correctly focused, because the film did not lie sufficiently flat in the camera's film channel. These sporadic anomalies occur because the film is quite thin and the backing paper is thin, and they can spring and buckle in odd ways in the sizable film gate as they react to increasing or decreasing humidity. They can also be slightly "rippled" when first stretched across the film channel after a long time curled around the film spool. None of these problems is imaginary, but none is so serious as to prevent 120 roll film from being a mainstay of professional photographers throughout the world.

Four standard image sizes are prominently associated with 120 roll film:

4.5 × 6 cm (1⅝" × 2¼")	16 exposures per roll
6 × 6 cm (2¼" × 2¼")	12 exposures per roll
6 × 7 cm (2¼" × 2¾")	10 exposures per roll
6 × 9 cm (2¼" × 3¼")	8 exposures per roll

The above frame sizes are nominal, which is why the metric and English dimensions do not agree exactly, and why you will seldom measure an actual film frame and find it more than an approximation of the appropriate dimensions. Furthermore, the numbers of exposures per roll are also nominal, and different models of different cameras may print one more or less than the

Relatively large 6 × 6 cm negative can yield excellent sharpness, tonality, and freedom from grain, even with high-speed film. "Secret" is that less enlargement is required.

number indicated, according to the interframe spacing and other film-transport variations.

As a class, cameras using 120 roll film are necessarily larger and heavier than 35 mm cameras. This is especially true of models with interchangeable lenses and accessories that enable them to approach the versatility of the more elaborate 35 mm camera systems. The individual rolls of film are larger but provide fewer pictures than the longer 35 mm lengths. And the 120 cameras are generally (but not always) more difficult to use and carry over long periods of time because of their greater weight and bulk. Furthermore, the extraordinary variety of film types available to 35 mm users is not paralleled in 120, which is somewhat weak in exotica.

At this point, the practical photographer has to ask if, in fact, the 120 camera, with its drawbacks, can do anything that cannot be done more easily with a 35 mm camera of equivalent quality and versatility. The very compelling answer is that the 120 camera will make substantially the same type of picture as the 35 mm camera, but it will do so on a substantially larger piece of film. This may translate into higher technical quality when extreme enlargement of the image is required, easy viewing with the naked eye, and a more practical, although still difficult, film size for a retoucher to work on. To the professional photographer, who must take such factors into consideration, 120 film provides specific solutions to specific problems. For most nonprofessional photography and for much professional photography, though, the 35 mm format has more to offer.

220 ROLL FILM

The 220 roll of film was intended to double the number of exposures a photographer could make with medium-format roll film. It is essentially a double-length strip of film the same width as 120, but with no backing paper. The leading and trailing ends of the film strip are glued to opaque paper leader and trailer lengths, which protect the film from light while wound on a spool before and after exposure. The spool is the same size and type as used with 120 film. The double-length 220 roll fits this spool easily, as there is no backing paper to take up space.

Although 220 roll film will fit into any camera designed for 120 film, there are practical reasons for using it only in cameras or film magazines specifically designed with 220 in mind. Most current medium-format roll-film cameras are equipped to use 220 film as well as 120, but older models may not be. Because 220 film has no paper backing, it will be fogged if it is used in a camera or magazine with viewing ports for inspecting frame numbers or index marks printed on 120 roll film backing paper.

The frame counters of cameras designed for 120 only do not count high enough to accommodate the extra lengths of 220 film, and some film transport mechanisms disengage after cycling the number of times required to run off a 120 roll. Admittedly, these problems may sometimes be circumvented through improvisation. However, there is no easy way to stop 220 film from "floating" in the the film channel of a camera intended for use with 120. A 120-only film channel is deep enough to accommodate both the film and a layer of backing paper. A thickness of film only, as with 220, is a loose fit, and the film can shift back and forth excessively in the film plane, which can impair image sharpness.

Cameras and/or film magazines designed for compatibility with 220 film have either no viewing ports or ones that can be closed lighttight, and frame counters and advance mechanisms that will handle the 220 film's extra exposures. And the camera or magazine film channel may be adjusted to the proper depth for either 120 or 220 film.

Primary users of 220 film seem to be portrait photographers and the professional "candid men" who shoot weddings and other social events. They like the advantage of being able to reload half as freqently as with 120 film, while using the same relatively handy cameras producing satisfactorily large negatives for the purpose. Unfortunately, only a few film types are spooled in 220. Even the Kodak photographic products 1977–1978 catalog listed few enough 220 films to count on the fingers of one hand. At present, all film available in 220 can also be obtained in 120 form, but most films available for 120 cannot be found in 220 size.

OTHER PAPER-BACKED ROLL SIZES

Besides 120 roll film, five other sizes of paper-backed film on flanged spools are still available, although they are becoming rare. They are mentioned here because very large numbers of cameras were made for them in the past, and some are still available in good condition on the used-camera market. Bear in mind that these are essentially obsolescent film sizes offering very little choice in film types, and that production of these sizes is subject to attrition by reduced demand. Except as noted in the accompanying table, these frame sizes are not generally given in metric units in the U.S.

Because quite a few appealing cameras of high quality were made for 828 and 127 film, it's worth mentioning a problem inherent to both sizes. The film spools for 828 and 127 have extremely slender cores to allow a maximum amount of film to be wound into a small-diameter roll. This means that the film and backing paper are held in a very tight spiral near the core, which contributes to problems of film flatness in the camera. The result may be pictures that are inexplicably unsharp, despite a good lens and careful focusing.

828	
28 × 40 mm	8 exposures per roll
127	
$1\frac{3}{16}'' \times 1\frac{9}{16}''$	16 exposures per roll
$1\frac{5}{8}'' \times 1\frac{5}{8}''$ (4 × 4 cm)	12 exposures per roll
$1\frac{5}{8}'' \times 2\frac{1}{2}''$	8 exposures per roll
The $1\frac{5}{8}'' \times 1\frac{5}{8}''$ format is sometimes referred to as the "Super Slide" size.	
620	
$1\frac{5}{8}'' \times 2\frac{1}{4}''$ (4.5 × 6 cm)	16 exposures per roll
$2\frac{1}{4}'' \times 2\frac{1}{4}''$ (6 × 6 cm)	12 exposures per roll
$2\frac{1}{4}'' \times 3\frac{1}{4}''$ (6 × 9 cm)	8 exposures per roll
The 620 film is the same size as 120 film, but the 620 spool is larger, and the films are therefore not interchangeable.	
616	
$2\frac{1}{8}'' \times 2\frac{1}{2}''$	16 exposures per roll
$2\frac{1}{2}'' \times 4\frac{1}{4}''$	8 exposures per roll
116	
$2\frac{1}{2}'' \times 4\frac{1}{4}''$	8 exposures per roll

70 mm FILM

Like 35 mm, 70 mm film intended for use in general-purpose still cameras is perforated along each edge for sprocket-drive transport through the camera, and it is bare film with no backing paper. The 70 mm designation refers to the film width, including the perforations. And again, like 35 mm, 70 mm film is available in two basic forms: metal daylight-loading magazines and long 100-foot rolls for darkroom loading into suitable magazines.

The factory-loaded 70 mm film magazine resembles an oversized 35 mm magazine, and holds 15 feet of film. This is enough for approximately fifty 6 × 7 cm ($2\frac{1}{4}'' \times 2\frac{3}{4}''$) or seventy 6 × 6 cm ($2\frac{1}{4}'' \times 2\frac{1}{4}''$) frames. Interchangeable 70 mm film backs or magazines for medium-format cameras that accept them generally hold two 70 mm daylight magazines. Film is fed from a

Interchangeable Hasselblad 70 mm film magazine is larger than motorized Hasselblad EL/M 6 × 6 cm SLR to which it is attached. Magazine holds 100 feet of film for more than 500 exposures without reloading. A smaller 70 mm film back accepts daylight-loading magazines holding 15 feet of film. Courtesy Braun North America.

full magazine, across the film gate and into an empty, or take-up, magazine. This avoids running the film strip through the camera twice. Empty film magazines may be reloaded in the darkroom for economy, to obtain nonstandard lengths of film, or to take advantage of film types not factory-packed in daylight magazines.

The main advantage of 70 mm film in still photography is extended shooting capability coupled with medium-format frame size. Disadvantages are relatively high cost of factory-loaded magazines, comparatively heavy, large interchangeable film backs and roll holders, which can be awkward in hand-held photography, relatively limited choice of film types in factory-loaded magazines, and relatively few processing laboratories properly equipped to handle it well. To the professional photographer who must make a large number of photographs in a short time to capture a certain mood, look, or expression, as in fashion or beauty photography, the advantages of 70 mm film far outweigh its disadvantages.

At the risk of confusing what seemed simple enough, it should be noted that 70 mm film is also used in a variety of special-purpose applications in high-speed, wide-field, and movie cameras. Consequently, in long-roll form, it is available in two distinct perforations (Type I and Type II) and a bewildering variety of spool types, darkroom-load or subdued-light-load rolls, and emulsion-in or emulsion-out windings. It is also available in an unperforated version. The practical significance of this is simply to make sure that the film you stock up on for the 70 mm format meets the specifications for the camera/magazine/roll holder in which you intend using it.

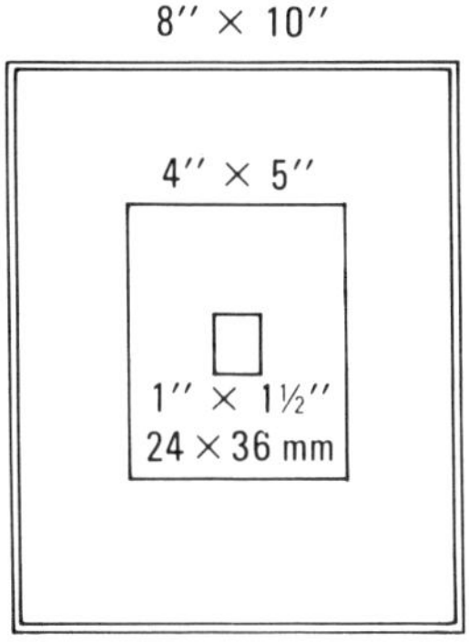

Relative sizes of 35 mm, 4″ × 5″, and 8″ × 10″ formats indicate dramatic differences in image-recording area. To make 8″ × 10″ print, 35 mm frame must be enlarged 8X, the 4″ × 5″ frame only 2X, and 8″ × 10″ original requires no enlargement.

SHEET FILM

As the name implies, sheet film is film that has been cut into sheets of standard size. In the United States, standard sizes range from 2¼″ × 3¼″ to 20″ × 24″, but the most popular sizes are 4″ × 5″ and 8″ × 10″. An intermediate 5″ × 7″ size has been losing ground in recent years, as many photographers feel that it combines the drawbacks of a very large, heavy camera with an image size that does not offer dramatic advantages over 4″ × 5″. Basically, all sheet film, regardless of dimensions, is handled similarly, in a manner that has not changed appreciably since the early days of photography.

Sheet film is loaded into a camera in a film holder, which is usually designed to hold two sheets of film, one on each side. The holder is somewhat like two picture frames mounted back to back. The opposite sides are separated by a rigid black back panel that is common to both. Each side has frame-like "rails" forming the edges of an opening corresponding to the film size. The top frame edge, which runs across the short dimension of the film, has a narrow slot lined with soft, light-trapping material. A stiff black dark slide slightly larger than the image aperture passes through the slot and fits grooves in the frame edge along the sides and at the bottom of the holder. When the dark slide is pushed all the way into the holder, it provides a lighttight seal over the film area. The bottom edge of the frame is hinged to open outward when the dark slide has been withdrawn far enough to clear the groove into which it fits in the bottom edge. When the dark slide has been partially withdrawn and the bottom edge opened, a sheet of film may be slipped into the holder so that thin retaining rails on the back panel hold the long edges of the film and position it. This must, of course, be done in a darkroom or other totally dark area. The bottom edge is swung shut, and held closed by sliding the dark slide fully into place. The opposite side of the holder is loaded similarly. Once the dark slides are in place, the holder is lighttight.

To make a picture, the film holder is inserted in the camera back, which forms a lighttight seal around it through a series of matching ridges and grooves plus heavy spring-clamp pressure. The dark slide is withdrawn from the side of the holder facing the camera lens, the exposure is made, and the dark slide is reinserted to cover the film. The holder is then removed from the camera back, and the entire process is repeated with the second side of the holder if a second exposure is desired. Most film holders have safety clips that prevent a dark slide from being pulled accidentally. And to reduce the likelihood of inadvertent double exposures on a single sheet of film, each side of a dark slide, near the top edge, is coded both visually by color and tactilely by small bumps or ridges. The photographer then disciplines himself always to insert the dark slide facing one way over fresh, unexposed film, and to reinsert it facing the opposite way when the film is exposed.

Obviously, the photographer using sheet film cannot shoot as rapidly as with a smaller-format camera, nor can he generally shoot as extensively. The holders are too large and too heavy to permit carrying very many on location. Furthermore, the holders are comparatively expensive, and the film itself is quite expensive, per shot, compared to smaller formats, dramatically so in terms of color transparency materials and processing charges. On the face of it, photography with large-format cameras and sheet film seems to present more problems than the photographer should be asked to bear. Even so, there is in progress a resurgence of interest in large-format photography that is spreading beyond the ranks of professional photographers to include serious amateurs. The explanation centers on two attributes of sheet films and the camera systems in which they are used: the additional area of the original and versatility.

The size of image-recording area is important to the photographer who wishes to record maximum detail with maximum fidelity, and who wishes the viewer of the finished picture to experience minimal sense of photographic materials and processes separating him from the original subject.

The size of the camera original becomes increasingly important as the size of the final picture increases. The more the camera original must be enlarged to produce the final picture, the less satisfactory the result is likely to be from a technical standpoint. A detail that looked tack sharp in the camera original when viewed with the naked eye, may look unsharp when enlarged five or ten times. The tonal transition that blends smoothly from a bright highlight to a deep shadow in the camera original may, under enlargement, take on a rougher, discontinuous look. The graininess of the film itself, which is seldom evident when viewing a camera original, may become prominent to the point of distracting the viewer's attention from the substance of the photograph when the image is enlarged appreciably. Increased film area alleviates these problems.

For the commercial photographer, large sheet film yields some other practical advantages. Retouching, which is the rule rather than the exception in making images for commercial purposes, is easier to do well on large originals (although it is often done on enlarged duplicates or prints, depending on the individual situation).

Where versatility is concerned, a great variety of general-purpose and special-purpose films are available in sheet-film sizes, and the cameras in which sheet film is used cover an extraordinary range of capabilities and applications. The cameras will be discussed in a later chapter, but suffice it to say that some can produce effects unattainable with current smaller-format cameras.

Aside from size, but related to it, sheet film differs physically from smaller-format rolls and strips. The base material on which the light-sensitive emulsion is coated is thicker for a sheet film, to prevent it from buckling and sagging out of position in the film holder. The thicker base also provides additional body for easier darkroom handling.

Because loading film holders, unloading them, and processing sheet film must be done in the dark (except for certain special-purpose films that may be handled under weak darkroom safelights), each sheet of film is notched in a distinctive pattern of v-shaped and rectangular indentations on one edge, near a corner. The number of notches and their shapes and sequence indicate the specific type of film, so the photographer or darkroom technician can verify by feel that a particular sheet of film is, indeed, what it is supposed to be.

The notches also provide a positive guide to orienting the sheet of film correctly for loading in a film holder. By convention, the notches are located so that they will be felt at the right top

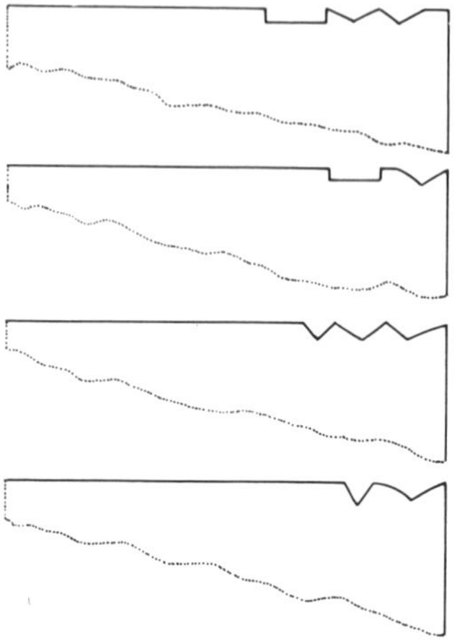

Code notches in sheet film permit identifying film type by feel in darkroom. When sheet of film is held with notches at top right, as shown, technician knows light-sensitive emulsion is facing him.

edge when the sheet of film is held with the light-sensitive emulsion facing toward the darkroom worker. This helps avoid the problem of discovering, after shooting an assignment, that the holders were loaded with the emulsion facing the rear of the holder rather than the camera lens.

Although, as mentioned earlier, sheet film is available in sizes as small as 2¼″ × 3¼″, this discussion has been predicated largely on the assumption that the world of sheet film really begins with the 4″ × 5″ size.

Most cameras that use sheet film are designed to be used from a tripod, and usually cannot be used hand-held. This applies even to the smaller ones that accept 2¼″ × 3¼″ film. Although the cameras that take 2¼″ × 3¼″ film are admittedly smaller and lighter than models designed for larger film, as are the lenses and film holders, they are no faster to operate. They take just as long to set up, adjust, focus, and manipulate, and the film must still be loaded and exposed sheet by sheet. In exchange for moderately reduced weight and bulk of the photographic outfit, the photographer is making more than a moderate sacrifice in film area. In the case of 2¼″ × 3¼″ versus 4″ × 5″, the former provides approximately 7⅓ square inches of film as opposed to the latter's 20 square inches. Most 4″ × 5″ cameras will accept, or can be adapted to accept, accessory roll-film holders for 120 and/or 220 film. Thus adapted, they can produce medium-format originals should the need arise.

On balance, sheet film can yield photographs that are remarkably rich in detail and that render the tones and textures of the subject magnificently. The large formats are easy to retouch, are impressive, require little enlargement for most purposes, and tend to reproduce very well on the printed page. For the photographer intent on capturing spontaneous events and expressions in rapidly changing situations, sheet film is anathema. For the photographer working with models in a controlled studio environment, shooting architecture, or painstakingly designing an elegant still-life set, sheet film is the perfect choice.

INSTANT-PICTURE FILMS

Polaroid Corporation and Eastman Kodak Company are at present the only suppliers of instant-picture films. Polaroid films are not usable in Kodak cameras, and Kodak instant films will not fit Polaroid Land cameras. Polaroid offers a wider range of instant film types, including black-and-white print, black-and-white print plus reusable negative, and color-print materials. In addition, Polaroid produces numerous special-purpose films for graphic arts, scientific, and industrial applications. Kodak instant film is available in only a color print version at this writing.

Formats available in the Polaroid line-up range from obsolescent roll films for Polaroid Land cameras long out of production to their latest achievement: 8″ × 10″ sheet film that yields a magnificent color print with only a minute's processing time. The most popular general-purpose Polaroid film sizes and packagings are:

- 10-exposure pack, 3½″ × 4¼″ print size, 3⅛″ × 3⅛″ image area
- 8-exposure pack, 3¼″ × 3⅜″ print size, 2¾″ × 2⅞″ image area
- 8-exposure pack, 3¼″ × 4¼″ print size, 2⅞″ × 3¾″ image area
- Sheet film, 4″ × 5″ print size, 3½″ × 4½″ image area

The above are not the only sizes of Polaroid film, but they are the most widely used for general photography. It should be noted that professional photographers use considerable quantities of Polaroid film in conventional cameras by means of accessory roll, pack, or sheet holders. The rapid availability of the Polaroid image permits the photographer to check exposure, lighting, and overall appearance before making the final shot with conven-

Peel-apart Polaroid Land films require user to separate positive print from negative material after development. Inconvenience is more than counterbalanced by variety of instant films available in peel-apart configuration. Courtesy Polaroid Corporation.

tional film. In some cases, Polaroid black-and-white film that yields a fine-grain reusable negative in addition to the print does double duty for both test shot and final shot.

Kodak's instant color-print film is available only in a 10-exposure pack and produces a useful image area of 2⅝″ × 3⁹⁄₁₆″.

The outstanding advantage of shooting with instant-picture films is being able to view a finished photograph within seconds or minutes of making the exposure. The major disadvantages are

Eastman Kodak Instant Print Film pack contains ten sheets of color film and snaps into camera like a flat cartridge. Courtesy Eastman Kodak Company.

With Polaroid SX-70 Land color film for SX-70 and several other Polaroid models, dry, developing print is ejected from camera immediately after exposure, but image is not apparent for several minutes. Full development takes eight to ten minutes. Only one film is made for SX-70-style cameras. Eastman Kodak instant color film is somewhat similar in use, but not interchangeable. Courtesy Polaroid Corporation.

that the cameras designed specifically for general photography with instant films are essentially snapshot cameras of varying levels of sophistication, and therefore somewhat limited; the film tends to be relatively expensive on a per-shot basis; the image produced (except in the case of Polaroid's reusable-negative

General-purpose and special-use Polaroid Land instant-picture films are available in 4″ × 5″ size for use in large-format cameras. Each film packet daylight-loads into special holder, which also incorporates processing mechanism. Courtesy Polaroid Corporation.

materials) can only be enlarged by copying, which entails a perceptible loss in image quality; and the print that is the camera original is unique and irreplaceable, and thus must be handled and stored with greater care than a conventional print, which can be replaced at will as long as the original negative or transparency is in good condition.

Perhaps because of the deceptive ease instant films bring to the image-making process, they are not often considered as prime materials for "serious" photography. This is unfortunate, because the instant films available today are first-rate materials capable of producing very fine images when handled with respect. Certainly, from the standpoint of the noncommercial "art" photographer, the uniqueness of a print that cannot be replaced should prove no more terrifying than the uniqueness of a painting to the painter. For the neophyte photographer, instant-picture film exposed in a camera permitting some degree of manual adjustment is a superb learning device. And for a vast body of nonphotographers who nonetheless want pictures for personal or task-related documentation, instant-picture photography is hard to match for convenience and impossible to match with regard to assurance that the picture has, indeed, "come out."

3

Viewing and Focusing Systems

To make a satisfactory photograph, the photographer must be able to position the image of the subject accurately within the film frame and record it with sufficient sharpness to yield the degree of information the end use requires. The camera's viewing system and focusing system, which are often combined, provide the means to these ends. There are many different types of viewing and focusing devices, ranging from the rudimentary to the complex, and regardless of manufacturers' claims, no one system is ideal for all applications. Since the viewing and focusing systems have a strong influence on the ease or difficulty of using a camera in various situations, it's worth taking a careful look at some of the major types of systems in common use.

SIMPLE VIEWFINDERS

The simplest viewfinders are those found in cameras with fixed-focus or scale-focus lenses. In a fixed-focus camera, the lens is set at the factory to provide a reasonably sharp rendition of objects within a certain minimum/maximum distance range, and the photographer must restrict picture-taking to that range to obtain adequately sharp results. Scale-focusing cameras permit focus to be adjusted over a fairly wide distance range by estimating the distance to the subject from the camera, then setting the lens focusing scale to a number or symbol corresponding to the subject distance. Focusing accuracy, and thus image sharpness, depends on the photographer's ability to estimate the distance.

Viewfinders for fixed-focus and scale-focus cameras generally serve one basic function: They provide a means of aiming the camera accurately enough so that scene elements appear in the film frame in approximately the same relative positions they occupied in the viewing system. It does not require an elaborate system to meet that requirement.

WIRE FRAMES

Older cameras often used folding wire frames for viewing, which consisted of a small rear aperture to position the eye and a larger forward frame corresponding to the film format. The manufacturer regulated the distance between the frames to provide an angle of view approximating that of the camera lens. Such finders are simple, quick to use, provide a view as bright as the scene itself, and can be repaired or replaced easily and inexpensively if damaged. Ironically, this very elementary open-frame finder is now most likely to be seen as a comparatively expensive accessory called a "sportsfinder" for certain medium-format roll-film cameras, or as the only feasible aiming device for several very expensive ultra-wide-field cameras that produce extraordinarily wide-angle pictures.

OPTICAL FINDERS

A step up from the wire frame, the optical finder is usually built into the camera body, where it is protected from minor bumps and scrapes. The optical finder, in simplest form, consists of a small optical viewing system with an eyepiece at the rear. The photographer looks through it and sees the scene outlined to indicate what will be recorded on film. The viewing image is usually bright in a well-designed optical finder, and may appear either life-size or slightly smaller than when viewed with the naked eye. The simplest optical finders indicate what will be included on film by blocking out extraneous areas. More elaborate optical finders incorporate a "bright frame" that appears to float in space around the scene, permitting the photographer to view a slightly larger area than just the portion included within the frame. This can be an advantage when photographing sports or other subjects involving considerable movement, as the slight additional viewing field surrounding the frame lets you see a person or object a moment before it actually enters the field that will appear on the film frame.

Optical finders are also available as separate accessories for rangefinder cameras with interchangeable lenses. These accessory finders are precisely made with fields of view that correspond to the fields of various wide-angle and telephoto lenses, and some have been made with adjustable optics so that a single finder can be used with several different lenses ranging from wide-angle to telephoto. Although few modern camera systems require separate finders for viewing, the finders have retained a small measure of popularity. Some photographers use them as previewing devices to help determine what type of lens to use without having to try a succession of lenses on the camera before finding the one that provides the most suitable field of view.

Because optical finders built into camera bodies are located somewhat off the camera lens axis, the view they provide differs very slightly from what the lens itself sees. This difference in view caused by the physical separation between the finder and the lens axis is known as parallax. At moderate to long distances, the discrepancy between what the eye sees through the optical finder and what the film sees through the camera lens is usually insignificant. At shorter distances, however, parallax error may become pronounced and result in inadvertent cropping of the subject on film. This often shows up in the form of missing arms and heads. To prevent this, built-in optical finders sometimes display etched parallax correction lines or marks to supplement the principal frame. The marks or lines show how much to displace the frame relative to the subject when shooting at close distances to ensure that the subject will not undergo amputation or decapitation by parallax.

At close distances, separation between viewfinder (A) and lens (B) of range-finder camera causes parallax error, a discrepancy between what eye sees through finder and film sees through lens. Here, eye sees subjects (C) and (D) in alignment, but lens sees (D) as slightly to right of (C).

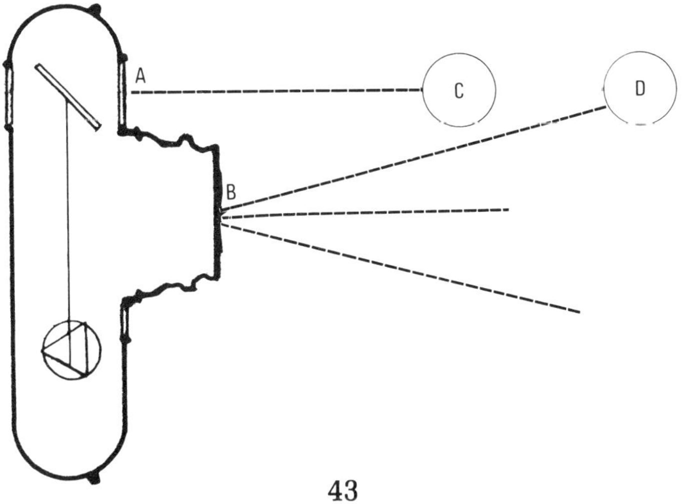

Optical finders are generally easy to see through even in dim light, they are compact and fairly simple in construction, and they provide a reassuringly direct view of the subject that is not interrupted during the cycling of the camera mechanism. Most people find optical finders comfortable and easy to use.

Although the primary function of the optical finder is to assure proper aiming of the camera, in many modern cameras it also serves as a basic information center containing displays or readouts pertaining to various camera functions. The data may be symbols, numbers, moving indicators, changing tints, light-emitting diodes (LED's), or nearly any conceivable combination of these. The intent is to provide important picture-taking information at eye level, so you don't have to take the camera away from your eye, possibly missing a good picture while doing so. Unfortunately, some camera designers get carried away with the information-center concept.

COMBINED RANGEFINDER/VIEWFINDER

A giant step up in convenience from the simple optical finder is the combined rangefinder/viewfinder. This consists of the familiar optical finder plus a prismatic rangefinder system coupled to the camera lens. The rangefinder allows focusing the lens accurately, without guesswork, by providing clear visual evidence that focus has been set correctly for a particular object. The rangefinding device usually is seen as a circular or rectan-

Bright viewing and quick focusing with rangefinder cameras make them ideal for capturing action.

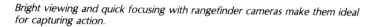

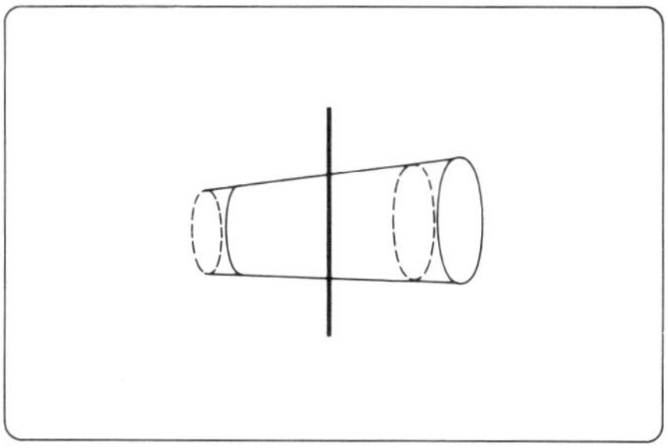

Rangefinder patch in center of viewfinder shows uninterrupted subject contour (solid line) when lens is focused on subject. When lens is not focused, secondary image of subject (dashed line) appears in addition to primary image. Focusing lens brings secondary image into coincidence with primary image.

gular tinted patch that "floats" in the center of the viewfinder field. When the camera is aimed so that the rangefinder patch is superimposed on the subject or part of the subject on which you wish to focus, operating the camera's focusing mechanism will cause a change in the appearance of the part of the subject covered by the rangefinder patch. A discrete subject detail, such as a mark or vertical line, that is unfocused will be seen double. As the focus improves, the extra, or secondary, image of the subject detail will move closer to its stationary, or primary, image in the rangefinder segment. When the lens has reached correct focus for the subject detail, the secondary image will be cleanly superimposed over the primary image, and the detail will look sharp through the rangefinder patch.

Since the coupled rangefinder is integral with the camera's viewfinder (except for some early cameras with separate rangefinder and viewfinder eyepieces), it provides fast, convenient focusing that is considerably more precise than can be achieved by guessing a distance. And since the rangefinder mechanism is not unduly large or heavy, it can be built into a camera without much penalty in overall size or weight. For available-light photographers who make photographs in dim surroundings, the rangefinder also offers the advantage of excellent potential accuracy even in near-darkness. And for most people, learning to focus by superimposing two distinct images is easy and provides positive results immediately. Nonetheless, the coupled rangefinder is not the ultimate answer to all focusing problems.

Rangefinders are generally unsuitable for two types of picture-taking: close-up photography and telephotography. It's easy to understand why. Bearing in mind that the rangefinder provides a view through two separated windows simultaneously, consider what happens when the subject is brought within inches of the camera lens. Maintaining the direct view of a focusing point through the viewfinder is not a problem, although parallax is, and soon becomes unmanageable. However, the viewing elements for the secondary image must swing more and more sharply to the side to keep the significant focusing detail in sight. Extreme movements of internal parts would be needed to produce an increasingly "cross-eyed" look at the focusing detail as the subject distance decreases. Although it might be possible to construct a rangefinder to meet this challenge, the cost of doing so would be a strong deterrent, and the parallax problem would still exist. Almost the opposite situation occurs with the use of long telephoto lenses. At the generally long distances at which these lenses are used, the necessarily limited separation of the rangefinder windows requires delicate and minute movements of the rangefinder parts to produce secondary image displacements that become, finally, too subtle for the photographer to evaluate. Solving these problems would entail increasing the size and cost of the rangefinder mechanism unacceptably.

Another inherent problem of rangefinder/viewfinder focusing and viewing is that the system is difficult to adapt to cameras that accept interchangeable lenses with widely varying fields of view. Although interchangeable-lens Leica, Contax, Canon, and Nikon rangefinder cameras reigned supreme for several decades with professional and advanced amateur 35 mm photographers, the range of lens focal lengths that could be used directly on the cameras without additional accessories was always relatively small. Although it is theoretically possible to design a viewfinder that could accurately delineate fields of view ranging from extreme wide-angle to extreme telephoto, along with a suitably versatile rangefinder, practical considerations of complexity, size, and cost render such a project questionable.

GROUND GLASS

Ironically, the focusing and viewing problems that are associated with rangefinders and optical viewfinders are solved or sidestepped neatly with systems based on one of the oldest viewing and focusing devices in photography, the ground glass. As the name implies, the ground glass is, in its classic form, a sheet of clear glass with one side finely ground to an even matte

Today's photographer using a view camera may drape a black focusing cloth over head and ground glass to keep ambient light from washing out the dim image, just as this poor soul did in 1861 depiction of "An Artist's Trials." Courtesy New York Public Library Picture Collection.

texture. In less classic form, it may be a sheet of glass or plastic with one surface textured by high-temperature, high-pressure molding. Either way, the result is a translucent screen on which the image cast by a lens may be composed and focused visually.

LARGE FORMAT

The simplest use of ground-glass viewing and focusing occurs in large-format sheet-film cameras, which hew closely to the elemental concept of the camera as a dark chamber with a lens at one end and a film-holding device at the other. A sheet of ground glass ruled to show the image area of the film format is mounted at the rear of the camera in a spring-loaded frame that positions it in the same plane that will later be occupied by the sheet of film. With the lens shutter open, the lens that will make the picture projects an inverted, laterally reversed image of the scene before the camera onto the ground glass. The photographer, usually with a black focusing cloth or an accessory hood over the ground glass to exclude ambient light, adjusts the distance of the lens from the ground glass until the image looks sharp where it is supposed to look sharp. He also adjusts the camera position to frame the subject properly within the outline of the film format, and adjusts the lens aperture as necessary to control sharpness in depth, with reference to the image on the ground glass. To make the photograph, the ground glass and its supporting frame are moved back from the rear frame of the camera, a film holder is inserted, and the ground-glass frame allowed to move forward again to clamp the film holder in place. The film in the holder is now in the same position formerly occupied by the ground glass during the viewing and focusing stage.

This focusing system combines great advantages with great disadvantages. When used in conjunction with a large film format, the equally large ground glass provides a big viewing and focusing image that is conducive to minute inspection of all parts of the image with the naked eye, or with a magnifier for critical control of focus. Since the lens that takes the picture is also the lens that forms the viewing/focusing image, there is no parallax problem, and the photographer has the reassuring knowledge that whatever is projected on the ground glass will be projected onto the piece of film. In short, the big, accessible ground-glass image provides the maximum opportunity to evaluate and control the image that will be recorded on film. Since the ground glass reveals whatever image is projected onto it, lens interchangeability is no problem, and the absence of parallax facilitates high-magnification work as in close-up or telephoto photography.

Unfortunately, the image formed on the ground glass is dim at best, and always much less bright than the scene. In bright light this is merely inconvenient. In subdued lighting, however, the ground-glass image may become so murky that only the brightest parts of the scene are distinct enough for focusing. This aggravates another aspect of focusing with a ground glass.

People with normal vision, or vision corrected to normal, almost without exception find it very easy to judge accurately when displaced images of the same object are brought into coincidence, as in rangefinder focusing. Ground-glass focusing, unfortunately, doesn't offer the eye such a clear-cut, on/off discrimination. Focusing with a ground glass involves watching the image make a smooth, stepless transition from some degree of fuzziness to whatever degree of sharpness the lens and circumstances permit. The photographer has to decide when the image looks *sharpest*, not just sharp. The nature of human vision is such that most people cannot make this discrimination quickly, easily, and accurately all the time.

Another problem with basic ground-glass viewing is that of working with an inverted, laterally reversed image. Photographers who have grown up with the system claim that an upside-down image laterally reversed presents the photographer with a desirably abstract set of shapes and tone relationships for compositional purposes, and that jarring aesthetic relationships are easier to spot.

Cameras that use basic ground-glass viewing and focusing are nearly always large, heavy, and tripod-mounted. Since there is no possibility of viewing or focusing through the camera when a film holder has been inserted in front of the ground glass, the system is unsuited to photography requiring freewheeling, spontaneous, fast coverage. It is ideally suited to photographic applications that benefit from a precise, studied approach, such as studio still-life work, highly detailed scenic photography, or architectural documentation.

SINGLE-LENS REFLEX

Early in this century, photographers concluded that if ground-glass focusing was good in big, slow, tripod-mounted cameras, it would be even better in smaller, faster-operating, hand-held cameras. This insistence on having the best of everything resulted in the development of the single-lens reflex camera, or SLR. The SLR sidesteps several of the major problems that occur with a rear-mounted ground glass by positioning the ground glass in the top of the camera, above the film chamber, and using a reflex mirror in the film chamber to bounce image-forming light from the camera lens up to the ground glass. The reflex mirror is hinged so that it may be swung out of the way of the direct light path from lens to film plane during the actual

Basic waist-level single-lens reflex (SLR) camera uses movable mirror between lens and film to reflect viewing/focusing image formed by camera lens to ground glass in top of body. Ground glass presents image upright but laterally reversed.

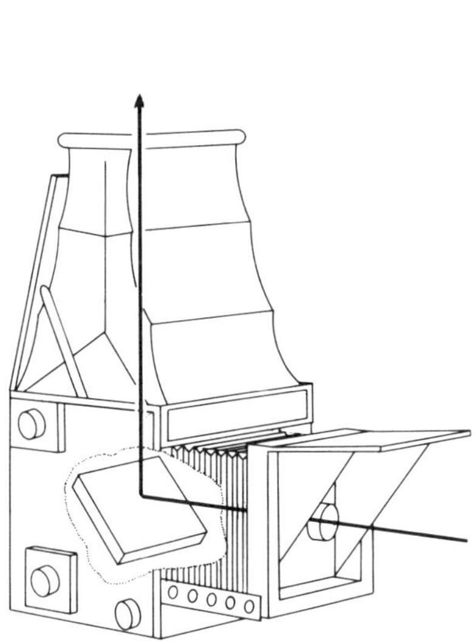

exposure. For viewing and focusing, the mirror locks at a 45° angle in the lens' light path and reflects light up to the ground glass. The ground glass, which is the same size and shape as the film frame, is located exactly the same distance above the center of the mirror as the film plane is located behind the center of the mirror. Light passing through the lens has to travel the same distance overall to reach either the ground glass or the film. Consequently, the same focusing adjustment needed to achieve image sharpness on the ground glass is appropriate to achieving image sharpness on film.

Not only did the basic SLR design combine ground-glass focusing and viewing with hand-held camera mobility, but it also provided an upright viewing image. The reflex mirror, in reflecting light to the ground glass, turns the image right-side up. In lieu of the black focusing cloth associated with studio-type cameras, early SLR's added the convenience of a collapsible, chimney-like viewing hood to prevent ambient light from washing out the relatively dim image formed on the ground glass. Sometimes a magnifying lens was incorporated into the hood for critical inspection of the ground-glass image.

Modern SLR cameras are among the most popular camera types, both in medium-format roll-film and 35 mm versions. Although modern SLR's are light years ahead of their predecessors in terms of mechanical and optical performance, convenience, and speed of operation, they still depend on a 45° reflex mirror to reflect a viewing and focusing image onto a ground-glass screen. However, most current SLR's use a five-sided prism, called a pentaprism, above the ground glass to transpose the viewing image so that it is laterally correct and unreversed. With a pentaprism viewfinder system, the SLR can be a very fast-handling camera while retaining the acknowledged advantages of ground-glass viewing and focusing, which are still as desirable as ever.

As SLR cameras have become both more complex and automated, the SLR finder area has begun to serve as a visual "master control center" for a variety of camera functions. In selecting an SLR, it is highly advisable to decide realistically how much subsidiary finder information is actually necessary for the types of photography you will be doing, and to reject finder displays that you find confusing or distracting. Be especially wary of data or function presentations that intrude significantly into the viewing/focusing area.

Modern SLR's have still not conquered the limitations of human vision, and many photographers using SLR's for the first time find that focusing with a ground glass does have to be

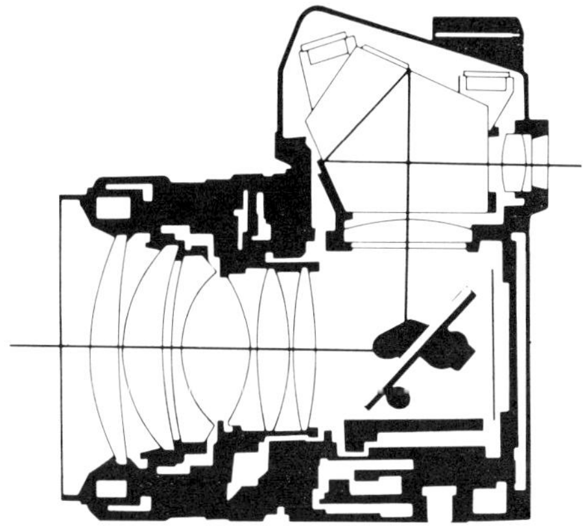

Diagram of Minolta SR-T 35 mm SLR shows light path (heavy line) through lens and viewfinder system. Image formed on ground glass is reflected by facets of pentaprism so that it appears oriented same as actual subject. Courtesy Minolta Corporation.

learned and does not come as quickly and easily as focusing with a rangefinder. It's fair to say that SLR cameras do not focus as quickly and positively as rangefinder cameras, nor do they present as bright a finder image. It's also fair to say that for most applications, these drawbacks are less significant than the real advantages offered by being able to compose and focus by observing the image that is actually being formed by the lens that will make the picture.

TWIN-LENS REFLEX

A third variation on the ground-glass theme occurs in the twin-lens reflex camera, or TLR. As the name implies, the TLR has two lenses and a reflex mirror. The two lenses are matched for focal length, and one is used to make the picture, the other for focusing. The bottom lens is the taking lens, and projects its image onto the camera's film plane. The upper lens is for viewing and focusing, and is mounted on the same panel that carries the taking lens. Both lenses are mounted with their optical axes parallel, so that both cover the same field. The upper viewing/focusing lens projects onto a fixed 45° reflex mirror that reflects the image-forming light onto a ground glass in the top of the camera, where the image appears upright and laterally reversed. The lower film chamber and the upper mirror chamber are sealed off from each other to prevent light from the upper lens from fogging film during the exposure. The standard viewfinder associated with TLR cameras is a folding chimney hood with built-in magnifier for critical focusing, but accessory eye-level pentaprism finders have been produced for some of the more elaborate models. Most TLR cameras are designed for use with medium-format roll film.

The TLR viewing/focusing system combines the major disadvantages of both optical viewfinders and ground-glass focusing. Since the viewing and taking lenses are separated, the TLR suffers from close-up parallax that limits its usefulness. Although some TLR's use automatically shifting frames or indicators linked to the focusing mechanism to provide parallax correction, there is still a difference in viewpoint between the two lenses that hampers precise composition at close distances. At the same time, the viewing and focusing image is comparatively dim, because of the limitations of through-the-lens focusing with a ground-glass screen, and it is laterally reversed unless a bulky, heavy, and expensive accessory pentaprism is fitted to the camera. Because the viewing lens must match the taking lens to assure compatible image size and focus, anyone attempting to make a TLR with interchangeable lenses must face the grim necessity of designing interchangeable pairs of lenses, not just lenses. Only one major manufacturer, Mamiya, has produced interchangeable-lens twin-lens cameras, and has thereby gained a loyal following among those photographers who feel that TLR's are uniquely useful for the type of work they do.

Equipped with a standard focusing hood, the TLR is not well adapted to following moving subjects because of its laterally reversed viewing/focusing image. Some twin-lens reflex focusing hoods incorporate hinged panels that swing up or down to convert the standard focusing chimney to a simple straight-through "sportsfinder," with small eye-centering rear opening and a larger front opening corresponding to the film format. As the ground-glass screen is not visible while using the sportsfinder, focusing must be done by estimation. A few TLR models have added a small mirror or prism to the sportsfinder arrangement to permit glimpsing a bit of the ground glass while using the open finder, thus allowing the photographer to follow action easily with the open-frame finder while retaining some ground-glass focusing capability.

A genuinely strong case for TLR viewing can be made by photographers who do a great deal of portraiture and/or flash photography. Unlike the reflex mirror of the single-lens reflex, which must swing out of viewing position to permit image-

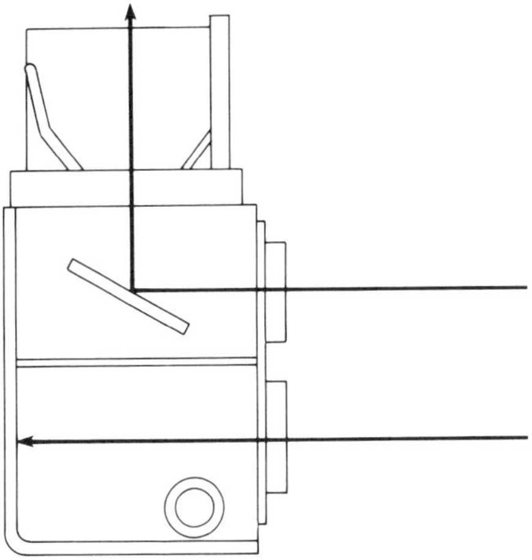

Lower lens of twin-lens reflex (TLR) camera forms image on film, while upper lens of identical focal length forms viewing/focusing image that is reflected by stationary reflex mirror to ground glass in top of body. Both lenses are mounted on single panel that moves fore and aft to focus. Image seen through waist-level hood is upright and laterally reversed.

forming light to reach the film during the exposure, the twin-lens reflex camera's mirror is mounted well away from the lens-to-film-plane light path and remains in viewing position at all times. The TLR thus provides uninterrupted viewing during the exposure, so the photographer can see if the subject blinked or moved suddenly, or if the flash failed to fire. It should be noted, however, that cameras with optical viewfinders also provide this advantage, plus a significantly brighter viewing image.

Generally, the viewing/focusing screens of TLR's are uncluttered with data displays and camera-function indicators because TLR's tend to be less automated than many SLR's. In the absence of so much automation, there is no need for elaborate systems to tell the photographer what the camera has "decided" to do at the moment.

Whichever system of viewing and/or focusing you find most appropriate to your needs and preferences, bear in mind that there is considerable variation in the way different manufacturers design and produce the same type of finder system. If you are about to buy a camera, compare similar models from several manufacturers to see if your eyes are more compatible with one than another. And be sure to include dim-light and bright-light comparisons. It can be surprising to discover that several finder systems that appear nearly identical in viewing and focusing convenience in bright light may be quite unequal in their abilities to cope with subdued lighting. Discovering the difference before you buy is preferable to discovering it afterward. You may also want to consider how easy it is to use the camera finder system while wearing eyeglasses, as finders can differ in this regard.

Because the camera's finder system is the most critical part of the machine in terms of allowing you to compose and focus accurately and quickly, and is therefore a key element in photographing your subject successfully, make as few compromises as possible in this area. After all, *seeing* is what photography is all about, and seeing easily and well through the camera is a giant step toward making good pictures.

4

Basic Shutter Types

The camera shutter shields the film from light until the photographer presses the shutter release, whereupon the shutter opens, exposes the film to light for a predetermined period of time, and closes again, shielding the film, when the desired time has elapsed. To do this, a shutter comprises two assemblies that work together: a movable light barrier and a precise timing device to control it. In the early days of photography when sensitized materials were relatively slow to react to light, exposure times were measured in minutes. The typical "shutter" consisted of a snug-fitting, lighttight cap to cover the front of the camera lens, the photographer's hand to remove it and replace it, and his pocket watch to time the exposure. With modern films, exposure times often involve hundredths or thousandths of a second, and the lens cap, hand, and pocket watch fall short of the required speed and accuracy.

Despite the profusion of camera types and sizes currently available, nearly all rely on one or the other of two basic shutter types, the leaf or iris diaphragm shutter and the focal-plane shutter. To be sure, there are innumerable minor variations, but the two dominant themes are instantly recognizable as such. And both shutter types are found, in versions ranging from stripped to elaborate, in cameras ranging from nonadjustable snapshot designs to highly versatile system cameras.

LEAF OR IRIS SHUTTER

The leaf shutter, often called an iris shutter, is composed of many thin, petal-shaped metal blades. They overlap, covering

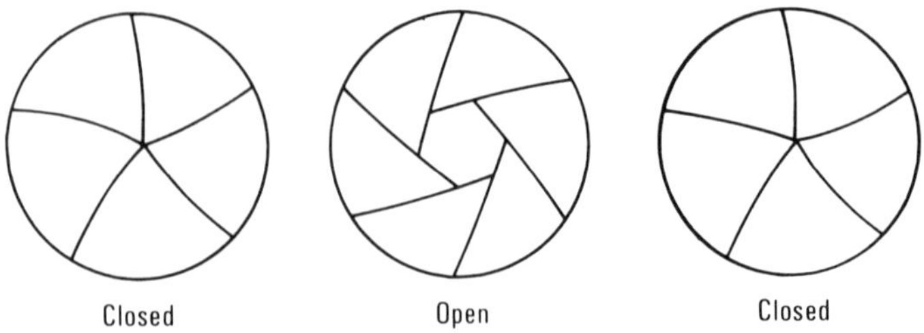

When leaf shutter is closed, blades overlap, barring entry of light. During exposure, blades swing away from center, opening concentrically, then swing back toward center to closed position. The instant the shutter opens, entire frame of film is exposed. Same operating cycle occurs at all speeds.

a circular area, and each is pivoted near the circumference of the circle so that it can swing outward. When the leaf shutter is tripped, the blades are swung on their pivots simultaneously, forming a circular opening as they move outward and clear of each other. As the blades continue to swing outward, the central aperture increases in size. When it has reached its maximum size, blade movement is arrested mechanically and the blades are held open by the shutter's timing assembly until the desired exposure time has been assured. The blades are then snapped shut, and the light is once again cut off from the film. Depending on the type of camera and the overall design criteria that must be met, a leaf shutter may be positioned in front of the lens, between the lens elements, or behind the lens.

Most leaf shutters provide a range of timed speeds from one second to 1/500 sec., although there are enough exceptions to make other minimum/maximum speeds quite normal. Other settings that are often encountered include "B" and/or "T,"

Leaf shutters may be positioned ahead of lens (A), between lens elements (B), or behind lens (C).

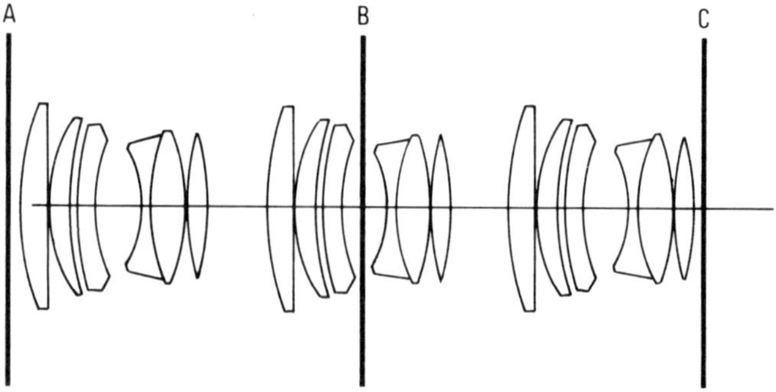

which indicate bulb and time, respectively. When set on "B" and tripped, the shutter will remain open as long as the shutter button is depressed, and will close when the button is released. At the "T" setting, once the shutter is opened by pressing the shutter release, it will remain open until the shutter speed selector is moved away from the "T" setting. "B" and "T" settings are used to make exposures longer than the slowest self-timed exposures the shutter can provide. The "B" setting is widely found on leaf shutters, the "T" setting is rare on current models, and finding both settings is uncommon except in shutters intended for use with large-format view cameras.

Three other settings that are sometimes encountered on leaf shutters are "M," "X," and "V," which are usually clustered together and selected with a single control. "M" is the synchronization setting for M-type flashbulbs, "X" is the synchronization for electronic flash, and "V" is a self-timer setting that delays shutter tripping for several seconds after the release has been pushed. Flash synchronization will be discussed later in this chapter.

Leaf shutters offer interesting advantages to both photographers and camera designers. Since the shutter assembly is generally quite compact and positioned somewhere within the lens barrel, the camera body itself can be smaller and uncluttered. Good leaf shutters tend to operate very quietly, producing an unobtrusive, soft click that does not call attention to the camera or the fact that pictures are being taken. They also function smoothly and generate minimal vibration, which if excessive could impair image quality. Because leaf shutters expose the entire film area simultaneously as soon as they begin to open, regardless of the shutter speed, they are unusually well suited to flash photography, particularly when flash illumination must be combined with ambient light.

Leaf shutters have their limitations. They generally do not provide speeds faster than 1/500 sec., and even the finest leaf shutters tend to operate more slowly than their markings indicate at the higher speed settings. They also are difficult and expensive to incorporate into interchangeable-lens cameras. If the shutter is positioned between the lens elements or elsewhere in the lens barrel, each lens must have its own built-in shutter, which increases the size, weight, and cost of the lens. If the shutter is built into the camera body at the lens mount, the physical size of the shutter opening imposes an inflexible limit on the optical design of lenses to be used on the camera, as well as limiting the camera's utility for close-up photography.

FOCAL-PLANE SHUTTER

In contrast, the focal-plane shutter is strong where the leaf shutter is weak, and vice versa. The focal-plane shutter is positioned within the camera body, as close as possible to the film plane. It is convenient to think of the focal-plane shutter as a set of two miniature window shades connected to a timing device. Typically, the "shades," called shutter curtains, that cover the film are made of black, opaque rubberized cloth, although some designs use lightweight titanium foil or metal blades. Regardless of the material employed, the manner of exposing the film is the same.

With the shutter cocked and ready, pressing the release button allows the first, or leading, curtain to move across the film gate in the camera. For a relatively long exposure of about 1/60 sec. or slower, the leading curtain runs across the film gate, exposing the entire frame of film to light entering the camera through the lens. After the appropriate time has elapsed, the timing device that governs the shutter releases the second, or trailing, curtain, which runs across the film frame and closes in a lighttight seal against the trailing edge of the leading curtain. The film is again protected from light. Tensioning the shutter draws both curtains *back* across the film gate together, so light still cannot strike the film.

The curtains operate somewhat differently when a high-speed exposure is required. Since it is impractical to drive the

A focal-plane shutter (A) is located immediately ahead of camera's film plane. Rear location and relative compactness keep focal-plane shutters from interfering with optics in interchangeable-lens designs.

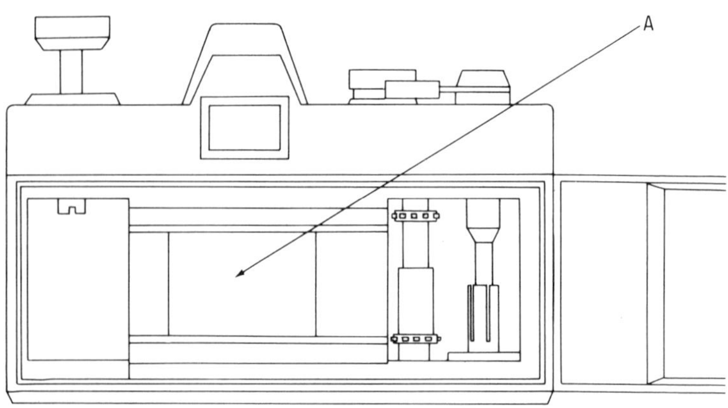

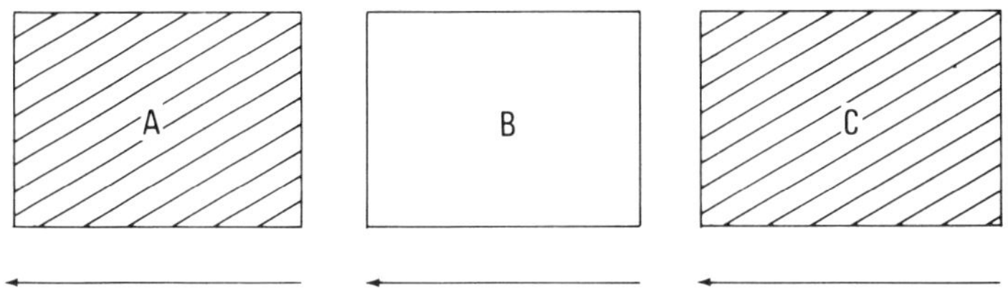

In slow-speed operation, first curtain (A) of focal-plane shutter opens roller-blind fashion to expose entire film frame (B). Second, or trailing, curtain (C) covers film again when proper time has elapsed.

curtains across the film gate fast enough to expose the film totally for a very brief interval such as 1/250 or 1/2000 sec., such high-speed exposures are made by exposing the film progressively, sweeping a strip of light across the frame. When the shutter is tripped, the leading curtain begins to traverse the film gate. When it has moved a few millimetres across the film gate the trailing curtain begins to move forming a narrow slit between the trailing edge of the leading curtain and the leading edge of the trailing curtain. When the slit is the proper width, the trailing curtain is released and follows the leading curtain across the film gate at the correct distance to maintain a constant slit width. As the slit races across the film gate, it allows a thin band of light to "paint" the image formed by the lens onto the film, section by section. The image is not recorded simultaneously on the entire piece of film at high speeds, but rather is "rolled" onto the film through the traveling slit between the shutter curtains. Depending on the shutter design, changes in shutter speed may be effected by altering the speed with which a slit of given width sweeps across the film gate, by altering the slit width while maintaining a

In high-speed range, focal-plane shutter's first curtain (A) sweeps across film frame, followed at preset distance by second curtain (C). Slit (B) between curtains "paints" narrow band of exposure across film frame rapidly, but only small portion of frame is exposed at any given instant. Entire film frame is not exposed simultaneously.

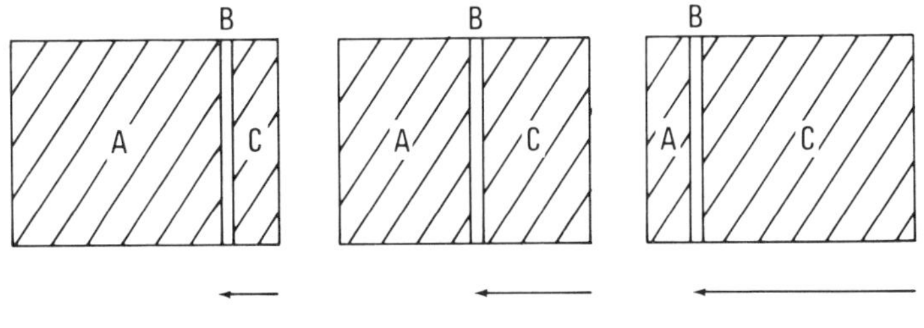

constant traverse time, or altering both traverse time and slit width as necessary.

The shutter-speed dials of nearly all cameras equipped with focal-plane shutters are engraved not only with numerical values for various shutter speeds, but also with the letters "B" or "T" (seldom both) and either an "X" or a distinctively color-coded mid-range shutter speed. As with leaf shutters, "B" and "T" are bulb and time settings, respectively. The "X" or color-keyed shutter speed signifies the fastest shutter speed that may be used when synchronizing an electronic flash unit. Depending on the type of shutter, this critical speed may be slower than 1/30 sec. or as fast as 1/125 sec. With most focal-plane shutters, electronic flash may be synchronized properly at any speed setting slower than the "X" speed, and with all focal-plane shutters, electronic flash cannot be used successfully at any setting faster than the critical speed.

As noted earlier, in its slow-speed range, a focal-plane shutter opens, exposes the entire piece of film, and then closes. In its high-speed range, however, it never exposes the entire piece of film to light at one time. An electronic flash unit produces a bright burst of light when triggered, but the duration of the burst is extremely brief. To be photographically useful, the burst of light must occur when the focal-plane shutter is completely open, exposing the entire frame of film. This condition exists only when the shutter is set to the "X" speed or a slower speed. At higher speeds, the entire film area is not exposed simultaneously, and therefore only a portion of the film frame will register an image produced by the flash. The inability of the focal-plane shutter to permit electronic flash photography at all shutter speeds is its major weakness in comparison to the leaf shutter. This drawback, however, is only significant to photographers who must often make flash pictures in which flash illumination is mixed with daylight or other strong ambient light, or who must make flash-only exposures in brightly lighted areas.

Generally, focal-plane shutters offer an extensive range of speeds, and the better made models provide good accuracy. Most focal-plane shutters are reasonably quiet, but they are not as quiet as leaf shutters. They also generate more vibration than leaf shutters. The great advantage of focal-plane shutters, which far overshadows their inconvenience, is their location immediately in front of the film plane, at the rear of the camera, and separate from the lens. This means that it is possible to interchange lenses and close-up accessories on the camera body without affecting the shutter and its operation. And the optical designer may work unhampered by size limitations or other considerations that would be imposed by having to build around a leaf-shutter system. This is one reason that focal-plane shutters are most often found in interchangeable-lens cameras and that leaf shutters are common in cameras with noninterchangeable lenses.

Focal-plane shutters used in 35 mm cameras are produced in two basic configurations: horizontal-run and vertical-run designs. Horizontal-run shutters traverse the long, 36 mm dimension of the frame, and vertical-run models sweep the short, 24 mm dimension. As a rule, the horizontal-run types use cloth or foil curtains and the vertical-run models use metal-blade curtains. The main practical difference between the two types lies in their abilities to synchronize electronic flash. Most current vertical-run focal-plane shutters can provide "X" synchronization up to and including 1/125 sec. Horizontal-run shutters usually provide "X" synchronization up to between 1/60 and 1/100 sec., depending on the individual design. Some vertical-run shutters are slightly more audible and vibration-prone than horizontal designs, although there are some exceptions to this statement.

TIMING

The shutters in recent and current camera models are calibrated to provide evenly stepped speed settings, with each higher speed yielding half the exposure time of the preceding step. (A typical speed series would run: 1 sec., 1/2 sec., 1/4 sec., 1/8 sec., 1/15 sec., 1/30 sec., and so on, to the highest speed. Some shutters may also be set between marked speeds to produce intermediate exposure times, but most cannot.) This provides two vital components of control to the photographer. By increasing or decreasing the time during which light can strike the film, the photographer can increase or decrease the level of exposure on the film to produce "correct" exposure, or some desired degree of overexposure or underexposure. The degree of exposure is an important in-camera determinant of the appearance of the final image. Furthermore, the time during which the shutter is open influences the way moving subjects will be represented on film. Longer exposures will show movement as a blur, while shorter exposures may freeze the subject movement and leave no hint in the photograph that motion was part of the original scene. The manner in which motion is recorded is clearly an important decision, both aesthetically and from the standpoint of conveying information to the viewer.

MECHANICAL TIMING

The timing assemblies that govern actual exposure duration of both leaf shutters and focal-plane shutters represent two different basic concepts. The older, traditional timing method is mechanical, and uses a clockwork-type gear train. Mechanical timing offers the advantage of familiarity, in the sense that mechanical shutters have been produced for well over a century in one form or another, and are known quantities to the people who design, manufacture, and repair them. A good-quality, mechanically timed shutter can be expected to provide good accuracy and dependability over a long service life. When and if repairs are needed, it's more than likely that any competent camera repair technician will be able to tackle them successfully. On the negative side, mechanical shutters tend to become less accurate as their timing gears and escapements become worn with use, clogged with dirt, or react to temperature extremes.

ELECTRONIC TIMING

More recently, electronic timing systems have begun to gain widespread acceptance. Electronic shutter timing promises, and sometimes delivers, a higher degree of accuracy and repeatability than mechanical timing. It has been claimed, with some truth, that electronic timing solves problems that are inherent in mechanical shutter timing devices. Unfortunately, electronic timing systems bring problems of their own, so their blessings are not unmixed. Certainly, it is easier to produce an electronic shutter-timing system of high potential accuracy than to produce a mechanical timing unit of equal performance. It is true, too, that an electronic timing circuit is not subject to mechanical wear, is not vulnerable to dirt, and is less vulnerable to extreme temperatures. It is equally true that the electronic timing device governs a mechanical shutter assembly that is subject to all the performance-limiting factors to which the electronic components are immune. As for repairs, the picture is highly variable. Some electronic timing circuits are cleanly designed and permit rapid replacement of defective components or modules, and others leave the repair technician a rat's nest of fine wiring.

The single greatest drawback to the electronically timed shutter, though, is the inescapable fact that it requires battery power. No matter how good the timing circuit and associated shutter may be, they will ultimately be no more reliable than the battery that powers them. The sad fact is that electronically timed shutters react to battery failure by losing all electronically timed speeds. To counter this problem, some are designed with limited mechanically timed operating capability. Typically, the photographer is left with the option of making long time exposures at the "B" setting or a medium-speed mechanically timed exposure at the shutter's "X" setting. Ironically, electronic timing assemblies' relative indifference to extreme heat and cold is not shared by the batteries commonly used to power them.

For most applications, it simply does not make much practical difference to the photographer whether the camera shutter is timed mechanically or electronically. Assuming equal shutter quality, neither type is likely to produce a perceptible variation in the final picture. From a camera design standpoint, though, electronically timed shutters do offer a significant advantage for use in auto-exposure cameras, which vary their exposure settings automatically in response to changing light levels. In cameras that achieve exposure automation by adjusting the shutter speed automatically, electronically timed shutters may be made to respond smoothly and continuously over their entire speed range, from the slowest speed to the highest. Thus, instead of yielding shutter speeds only at discrete time intervals, as with most mechanically timed shutters, the electronically timed shutter can be made to fire at precisely the shutter speed required for optimum exposure at a specific light level, even though that speed may be an odd, nonstandard fraction such as 1/173 sec. or 1/19 sec. This continuously variable speed-change capability can, indeed, allow making exposures that come closer to the theoretically ideal exposure level for the circumstances.

SHUTTERS AND FLASH

As touched on earlier in this chapter, leaf-type and focal-plane shutters differ markedly in their abilities to be synchronized with various types of flash illumination. Because flash photography can represent an important aspect of performance, it's worth taking a closer look at some of the differences and why they exist.

First, a distinction must be made between electronic flash and flash illumination produced by expendable flashbulbs. Although there are in fact many differences between these two flash sources, in terms of synchronization the important distinction is that an electronic flash unit produces a very brief burst of light immediately upon the completion of its firing circuit. A flashbulb produces a comparatively long-duration burst of light that does not reach maximum brightness for several milliseconds after the firing circuit has been completed. An oversimplified but useful explanation for these differences is that the electronic flashtube produces its short burst of light by the visible discharge of electrical energy, in what amounts to a standardized, repeatable artificial lightning flash. The flashbulb produces its longer burst of light by the actual burning of metallic filament wires or fine ribbons, which begin to burn slowly, then faster, reach a peak, and then are gradually consumed with a corresponding fall-off in light until all the combustible filler has been burned. Flashbulbs are subdivided into two main categories, M class and FP class. M-class bulbs are primarily intended for use with leaf shutters. They produce light in a manner that is comparable to the profile of a mountain ridge: a gradual rise to a peak, followed by a more gradual fall-off past the peak. FP bulbs are intended for use with focal-plane shutters, and their light output pattern is more like the profile of a plateau: a steep rise to a level that continues fairly flat and then decays in a gradual slope.

As noted earlier, the leaf shutter exposes the entire piece of film simultaneously the instant it opens. When the shutter's synchronization selector is set to "X" for electronic flash, it will complete the attached flash unit's trigger circuit when the shutter blades are fully open. Because the electronic flash fires so quickly, its entire light output will be photographically useful, as the shutter will be open longer than the flash will last. This basic sequence will hold true at all shutter speeds.

When the leaf shutter's synchronization selector is set to the "M" position, for flashbulbs, the firing circuit will be completed approximately 12 to 17 milliseconds before the shutter opens. This gives the gradual burning process in the bulb time to generate useful light output that will then coincide with the shutter's open period. Without this delay, the shutter might open and close again before the bulb has a chance to light up the scene. The owner's manual that accompanies a given camera will indicate the range of shutter speeds that may be used with "M" synchronization for various sizes of flashlamps.

With focal-plane shutters, the synchronization choice is normally "X" for electronic flash and "FP" for FP-class bulbs. At the "X" setting, the electronic flash unit's trigger circuit will be completed when the shutter is fully open, exposing the entire piece of film in the camera to the lightning-like flash of light. This presupposes that the shutter will be fully open at some point during the exposure. As noted earlier, a focal-plane shutter opens completely only when set to speeds no faster than about 1/30 to 1/125 sec., depending on the shutter design. At higher speeds, the shutter does not open beyond a narrow slit. Thus the focal-plane shutter's high-speed range will be unusable in conjunction with electronic flash exposures. In this respect, then, the focal-plane shutter compares quite unfavorably with the leaf shutter, which normally permits "X" synchronization at all speeds.

"FP" synchronization with a focal-plane shutter is analogous to "M" with a leaf shutter, in that the flash synchroni-

Fast-acting rangefinder cameras let you capture candid-picture-taking opportunities before they get away.

The limited depth of field of a 200 mm telephoto lens used at a wide aperture helped focus attention on the model. The long telephoto's compression of space also made background features appear closer than they were.

A 90 mm short telephoto lens aided tight cropping in the camera without intruding on this painter in Montmartre.

(Left) A slow shutter speed blurred a rider on a carousel as he whizzed past the camera.

This transparency, made with a rotating Hulcherama Model 120 panoramic camera, shows a view that is more than 360 degrees, inside Hardee's restaurant in Tokyo. The camera's self-contained, rechargeable battery powers 360-degree rotation rates ranging from 2 to 64 seconds per revolution. Manual switching permits covering more or less than 360 degrees when desired. The Hulcherama uses standard 120 film. (Photo by Simon Nathan.)

A 21 mm extreme wide-angle lens dramatically exaggerated perspective in this view of the Eiffel Tower.

PUSH
PUSH
大人の味
モカシェイク
OPEN
1030
2100
200YEN
180YEN
150YEN

In this photo of the Seagram Building, made with a 16 mm full-frame fisheye lens, maximum distortion of straight subject lines occurs in image areas that are farthest from the center. Straight subject lines are rendered reasonably straight near the center of the frame.

The pipe smoker is about 2½ inches tall seated, and his pet elephant stands at less than one inch. A 100 mm macro lens made the close-up shot at a convenient distance; far enough away not to cast shadows of photographer, camera, or lens into the miniature set.

In the studio, a 6 × 6 cm SLR is a good choice for beauty photography. For this shot, a 150 mm telephoto lens was used with a short extension tube to permit close focusing and tight framing.

(Above) Large-format view cameras are the best choices for still-life photography; A 4" × 5" or larger transparency provides ample film area to accurately record tone and texture, and view-camera movements allow great control over the way the subject is made to appear. (Below) SLR through-the-lens viewing and focusing lend themselves to precise composition and "designy" applications.

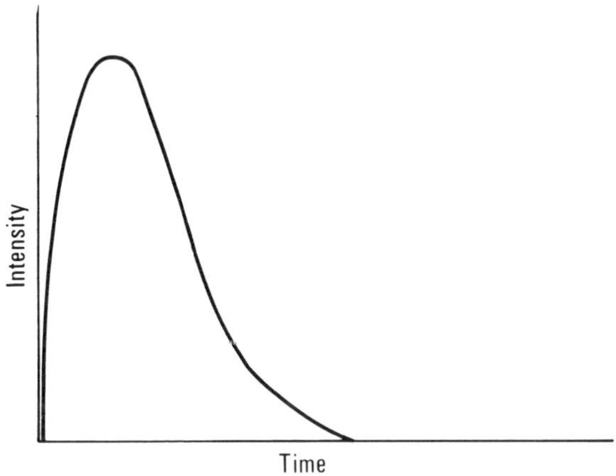

When an electronic flash unit fires, its light output rises rapidly to a peak, then falls off abruptly.

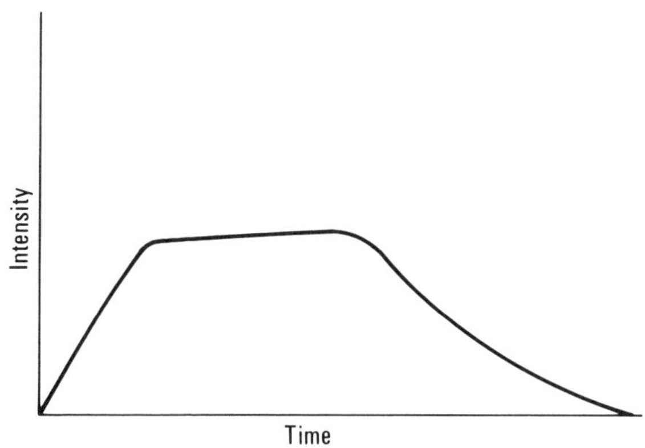

FP-type flashbulb designed for use with focal-plane shutters produces relatively stable "plateau" of intensity over extended flash duration. Photographically useful light is produced long enough to allow shutter's moving slit to expose entire film frame properly, even at high shutter speeds.

zation circuit is completed far enough in advance of the shutter's opening to ensure that the bulb is well into its burning cycle. The FP bulb is designed to provide even exposure while the focal-plane shutter traverses the piece of film. In this case, too, the owner's manual supplied with the camera will indicate the range of shutter speeds that may be used successfully with FP bulbs.

Unfortunately, variations in shutter design prevent any generalized figures from being universally applicable in this regard.

Incidentally, at shutter speeds of 1/30 sec. or slower and using the "X" synchronization circuit, most focal-plane shutters may be used successfully with most currently available flash sources, including electronic flash, FP bulbs, M bulbs, and AG-type all-glass miniature bulbs and their various derivations. Again, for specific information, consult the owner's manual for the camera as well as the tabular exposure and synchronization data furnished with the flashbulbs.

Although the shutter is a crucial component of any camera, and its design does influence the ease with which the camera may be used in certain circumstances, the subtleties that differentiate brands are of less consequence to the photographer than to the camera designer or repair technician. And most of the time, the film will never know the difference.

5

Lenses

The purpose of a camera lens is to transmit light reflected from the subject to the film inside the camera in such a fashion that the light will form a coherent image of the subject on film. In addition, the lens may regulate the amount of light that it transmits to control exposure and influence the appearance of the image with respect to the way depth is represented. Lenses usually permit adjusting focus to shift visual emphasis and clarity as required, and in interchangeable-lens systems, different types of lenses allow the photographer to select optical characteristics suited to specific situations.

FEATURES OF A LENS

Typically, a photographic lens is composed of one or more pieces of carefully ground and polished optical glass. Each piece of glass is called a lens element. A lens design may call for cementing together two or more lens elements with precisely matched surfaces into an assembly called a group. A group may also be a single element standing alone. The forwardmost element in the lens is called the front element, and the rearmost element is called the rear element. The various elements and groups that comprise a lens are assembled into a tube called the lens barrel.

APERTURE

In all but the simplest nonadjustable lenses, the barrel also contains a mechanism for adjusting the lens' physical aperture. The physical aperture is the actual diameter of the lens through which image-forming light may pass. To control the amount of light the lens transmits, the physical aperture may be

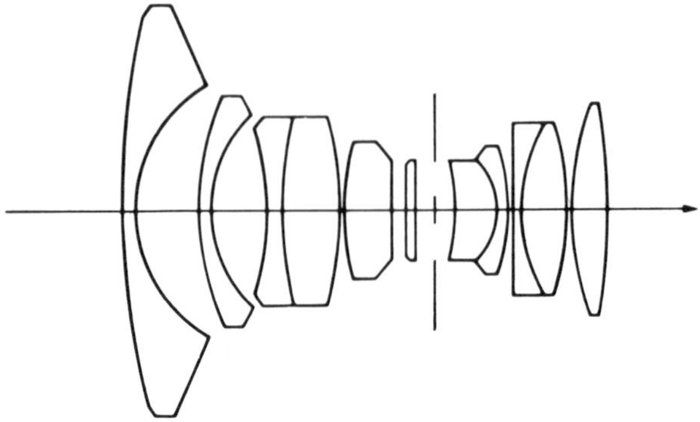

Complex 16 mm f/2.8 full-frame Minolta fisheye lens has 11 individual optical elements arranged in 8 groups. A group may consist of several elements cemented together, or a single element standing alone. Courtesy Minolta Corporation.

reduced by an iris diaphragm that is usually positioned between the elements, near the middle of the lens. The diaphragm is similar in construction to a leaf shutter, but is not connected to a timing module. Depending on the camera design, the diaphragm setting may be made manually by the photographer or automatically by the camera. Manual diaphragm setting is usually done with a ring or collar mounted concentrically on the lens barrel.

F/numbers, which describe lens speed, are determined by dividing focal length of lens by diameter of lens aperture. Here, dividing 50 mm focal length by 25 mm aperture equals 2. Lens has a speed of f/2.

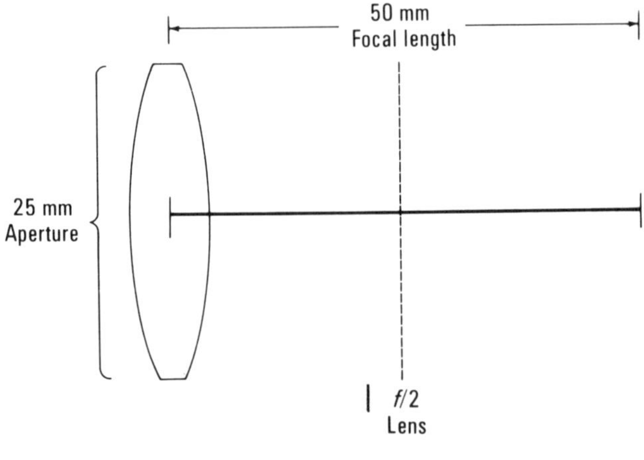

Lenses designed for use with modern single-lens reflex cameras may incorporate an automatic diaphragm mechanism controlled by the camera body. The purpose is to hold the diaphragm open for brighter viewing and focusing, then close it automatically to a preselected aperture at the instant of exposure, and allow it to open fully again immediately after the exposure has been completed. This is the most convenient type of diaphragm operation with an SLR camera. A mechanically simpler type called a preset diaphragm is also used for SLR lenses when the lens design or cost considerations preclude using an automatic diaphragm. The preset diaphragm consists of a freely turning control ring that adjusts the size of the lens aperture, and a click-stopped setting ring that you index to the desired aperture number. In use, you focus with the lens fully open, and close the diaphragm to the preselected aperture a moment before shooting by turning the control ring until it is stopped by the setting ring.

DIAPHRAGM MARKINGS

Standard diaphragm setting calibrations are expressed in *f*-numbers, and an *f*-number is also used to describe the maximum aperture, which is called the "speed," of the lens. A typical series of *f*-numbers on a normal lens for a 35 mm SLR might progress: *f*/1.4, *f*/2, *f*/2.8, *f*/4, *f*/5.6, *f*/8, *f*/11, and *f*/16. The smallest *f*-number represents the largest lens opening, and the largest *f*-number represents the smallest diaphragm opening. The

Depth of field (extent of sharpness from near to far in picture) can be controlled by lens aperture. With focus set for (A), wide lens opening produces little depth of field (upper bracket), and (B) and (C) are out of focus. A small lens opening yields greater depth of field (bottom bracket) that renders all three scene elements sharply.

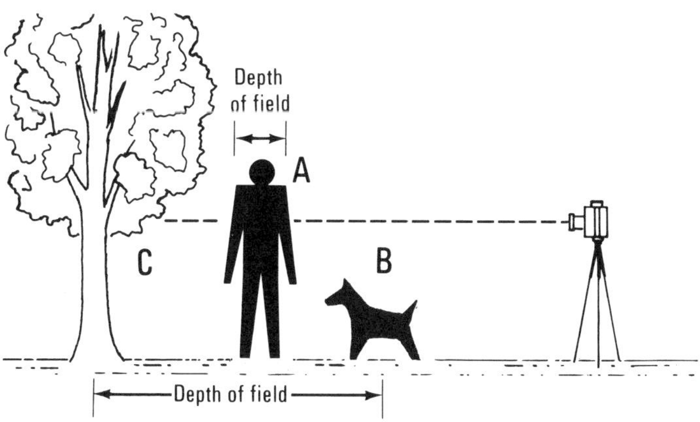

reason for this will be given later in this chapter. The spacing of the aperture settings is such that each smaller lens opening, or lens stop, admits one half the amount of light as the preceding setting. That is, *f*/2.8 admits one half the light of *f*/2, *f*/4 admits one half the light of *f*/2.8, *f*/5.6 admits one half the light of *f*/4, and so on through the range. This tallies with the progression of shutter speeds normally provided, which also decrease exposure time by 50 percent at each faster speed setting. Thus, for the purposes of exposure control, a one-stop (50 percent) reduction in the amount of light reaching the film in the camera may be achieved either by changing the shutter speed from 1/125 to 1/250 sec., for example, *or* by changing the diaphragm setting from *f*/4 to *f*/5.6.

DEPTH OF FIELD

Besides controlling exposure by regulating the amount of light that passes through the lens, the diaphragm has another pronounced effect on the final picture. The diaphragm setting affects the depth of field in the photograph. Depth of field is the amount of the scene ahead of and behind the principal subject that looks sharp in the picture. When we focus a camera on a person several feet away who is standing in front of a scenic attraction, we generally hope that the sharpness in depth will be sufficient to see both the person and the scenery clearly in the picture. In other words, we want the photograph to benefit from great depth of field. And sometimes, we may wish to photograph a person or object with the least depth of field possible in an attempt to blur everything nearer or farther than the subject so as to rivet the viewer's attention on the subject. The diaphragm setting control provides the flexibility to achieve these effects.

Large lens openings provide the least depth of field and small lens openings yield the greatest depth of field, all other conditions being equal. Assuming suitable light, then, we might choose *f*/11 or *f*/16 to make the picture in which we wanted both the person and the scenery sharp, and we might pick *f*/1.4 or *f*/2 for the picture in which we wanted the subject sharp and everything else noncompetitively soft. A handy way to remember the relationship between *f*-numbers and depth of field is to remember that doubling the *f*-number approximately doubles the depth of field with a given lens at a specific focusing distance. That is, *f*/8 will yield about twice the depth of field as *f*/4, and *f*/16 twice as much as *f*/8.

FOCUSING

Except for lenses built into fixed-focus cameras, lenses for cameras with built-in focusing movements, and lenses designed for use with special focusing mounts or accessories, most lenses for general-purpose cameras have a focusing mechanism built into the lens barrel. Most often it consists of a large, internally screw-threaded collar, or helix, that, when rotated, moves the lens elements closer to or farther from the film, depending on the direction of rotation. When the lens is at its closest distance to the film, it is focused for the most distant subjects, and will record with reasonable clarity subjects as far away as the eye can see clearly. At this focus setting, a lens is by convention considered to be focused on "infinity." To focus on closer objects, the lens must be moved progressively farther from the film as the camera-to-subject distance decreases. Depending on the design of the camera and/or lens, the closest feasible focusing distance may range from 100 feet or more for large telephoto (telescopic) lenses to such a close distance that the subject actually is in contact with the surface of the front element of the lens. As a rule, to which there are many exceptions, normal lenses for rangefinder cameras and cameras with noninterchangeable lenses focus down to approximately 2 to 3 ft, and normal lenses for SLR cameras often focus as close as 12 to 18 in. without accessories.

FOCAL LENGTH

An important descriptor of photographic lenses is the focal length, which refers to the actual distance from the camera's film plane to the lens' nodal point when the lens is focused at infinity. Focal length is usually expressed in millimetres or centimetres, although focal lengths of large lenses for view cameras are sometimes given in inches. *F*-numbers are derived by dividing the lens' focal length by the diameter of the diaphragm opening. For example, a lens with a focal length of 50 mm and a maximum aperture that measures 25 mm in diameter would have a maximum aperture of *f*/2 (50 mm divided by 25 mm equals 2). By convention, this lens would be described quickly as a "50 mm *f*/2" lens. Following the same basic calculations, it is easy to see that a 100 mm lens would require a maximum aperture of 50 mm diameter to achieve an *f*/2 designation, and a 200 mm lens would have to have a maximum aperture of 100 mm to be an *f*/2 lens. These examples indicate that the longer the focal length of a lens, the less likely it is to have great light-gathering ability, because of the size and weight limitations imposed by the necessity for outsized glass elements appropriate to the increasingly large apertures needed to achieve a low *f*-number.

The focal length of a lens bears a direct relationship to the size of the image it projects on film of a subject at a given distance. The longer the focal length, the larger the image will be. Assuming that the size of the film frame remains constant, long-focal-length lenses will produce large, magnified, or telescopic images, while short-focal-length lenses will yield small, minified images. Lenses with a moderate focal length will produce images of moderate size that look much as the original scene looked to the unaided eye. Such lenses are called normal or standard lenses.

A *normal* lens for a given film format usually has a focal length that is approximately equal to the length of the diagonal of the film frame. In fact, there may be some variation from format to format as to how closely the conventional normal focal length corresponds to the format diagonal, but it is generally close enough to be useful as a rule of thumb. For example, the full-frame 35 mm format measures 24 × 36 mm and has a diagonal of approximately 43 mm. According to the rule, a normal lens for a 35 mm camera should have a focal length of about 43 mm. Actually, normal lenses for 35 mm cameras are clustered in the 50–55 mm range for interchangeable-lens cameras and in the 40–

Normal focal length for a given film size is approximately equal to diagonal of film format. For 4″ × 5″ film, with 6.4-inch diagonal, normal focal length is about 150 mm, or 6 inches. The 35 mm format, with 43.3 mm diagonal, is associated with normal focal lengths from 40 mm to 58 mm.

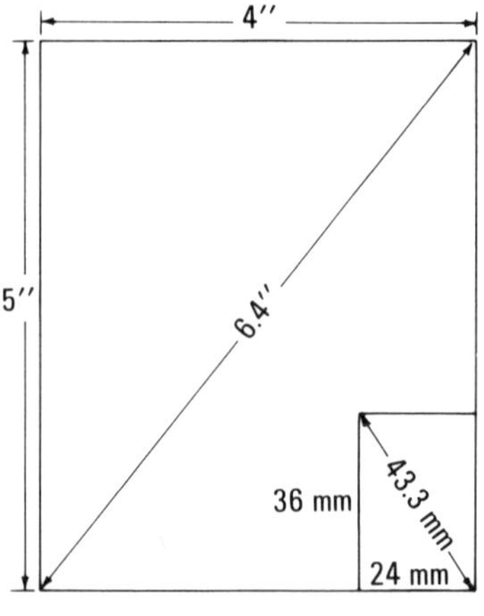

Covering power is size of lens' image circle relative to film frame. Lens with image circle (A) that covers 35 mm format falls far short of covering 4″ × 5″ negative. Image circle (B), which just covers 4″ × 5″, would be grossly excessive relative to 35 mm frame.

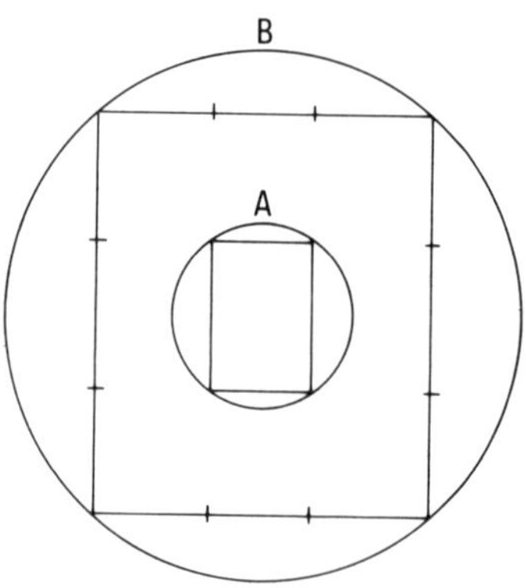

Photographs made at fixed distance from subject show increasing image size with increasing lens focal length. Minolta lenses were used. Courtesy Minolta Corporation.

7.5 mm circular fisheye

16 mm full-frame fisheye

21 mm extreme wide-angle

28 mm wide-angle

35 mm wide-angle

50 mm normal lens

100 mm moderate telephoto

200 mm telephoto

800 mm catadioptric extreme telephoto

50 mm range for noninterchangeable-lens cameras, with a few exceptions in both categories. With 6 × 6 cm cameras, the nominal film diagonal is approximately 80 mm, and most normal lenses for this format range between 75 mm and 80 mm. The nominal diagonal of the 8″ × 10″ view camera format is approximately 12.8 inches, which corresponds to the 12-inch focal length conventionally accepted as normal for this format.

A lens that is substantially longer than the standard focal length for a given format is called a *long-focus* or *telephoto* lens, and is used to fill the film frame with a larger image of the subject than could be obtained with a normal lens. Less subject area will be shown on film, but what is shown will be quite large. The terms long-focus and telephoto are popularly used interchangeably, although technically they refer to distinctly different optical solutions to the basic challenge of making a larger image fill the film frame. Without getting involved in technicalities, suffice it to say that if you compare a true telephoto lens with a true long-focus lens of the same focal length, the telephoto will be somewhat shorter.

A lens that is significantly shorter in focal length than the standard lens for a given format is called a *wide-angle* lens. A wide-angle lens is used to fill the film frame with a larger area of the subject than the normal lens can fit into the frame. To do this, each object in the scene must be rendered smaller on film than it would be with a normal lens. Thus the wide-angle lens reduces the size of subjects at a given distance from the camera, but includes more of them in the picture.

It is worth noting that focal length alone does not indicate whether a lens is a normal design, a telephoto, or a wide-angle. The reason lies in another aspect of lens design: covering power. To determine that, you must know not only the focal length, but also the film format with which the lens is to be used. For example, a 50 mm lens could be a telephoto relative to the 110 film frame, a normal lens relative to the full-frame 35 mm format, a wide-angle relative to the 6 × 6 cm format, and a more extreme wide-angle relative to the 6 × 7 cm frame. While a 50 mm lens designed as a wide-angle for a 6 × 7 cm camera might be used as a normal lens for a smaller format in theory, in practice that is not likely to occur, and the reverse situation is essentially out of the question.

NONINTERCHANGEABLE-LENS CAMERAS

Most cameras with noninterchangeable lenses are fitted with lenses in the normal-focal-length category, although a few

35 mm cameras have lenses that lie somewhere between wide-angle and normal. Since lenses with a normal focal length produce pictures that include a subject area corresponding quite closely to what we see when viewing the scene directly, they are very useful for a wide variety of situations. They produce pictures with a broad enough view to handle outdoor scenery, yet can be used at close enough distances, without exaggerating perspective too seriously, to make at least half-length semi-close-ups of standing people. From the horizon to the half-length figure covers a lot of ground, and most everyday photographic situations are handled easily with a normal lens. The same comments obviously apply to normal lenses used on interchangeable-lens cameras, too.

INTERCHANGEABLE-LENS CAMERAS

As useful as it is, the normal-focal-length lens cannot cope with all situations. Therefore, interchangeable lenses are available for many cameras to extend their vision. The fastest, most convenient means of attaching an interchangeable lens to a camera body is with a *bayonet mount*, and the bayonet mount, in one form or another, has virtually swept the field of 35 mm and medium-format roll-film cameras. The main drawback of the bayonet mount, which is more theoretical than real for most photographers, is that heavy use with frequent lens changes may, over the years, cause sufficient mechanical wear of the mount surfaces to affect the precision with which lenses seat on the camera body.

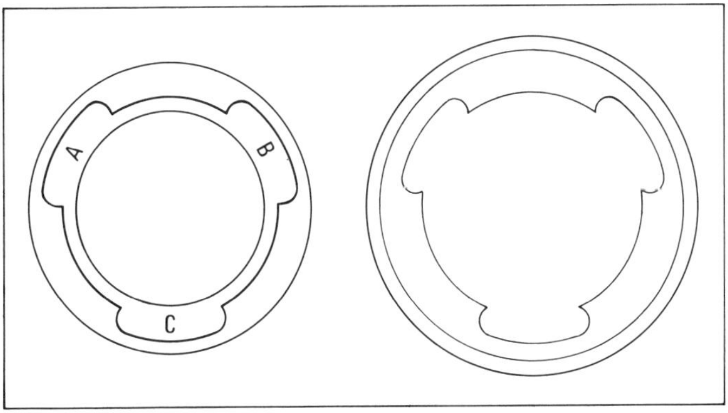

Bayonet lens mounts allow fast, positive lens interchanging. Lugs (A, B, C) projecting radially from rear of lens pass through matching clearance cuts in camera body's mounting flange. Twisting lens traps lugs behind projecting sections of flange, securing lens to camera body.

An older method of interchanging lenses that is still encountered although rarely incorporated into current-production models entails use of a *screw-in* mount. The rear fitting of the lens is a threaded ring, and the camera mounting flange is threaded to receive it. The lens is screwed into position on the camera body to a snug but not excessively tight fit.

The screw mount was long championed because of its simplicity, economy, and durability. Over extended use, the screw mount will continue to allow firm seating of the lens on the camera, as all but the most drastic thread wear may be compensated for by rotating the lens a bit more until it fits snugly in place. Practical drawbacks of the screw-mount system include slow removal and mounting of lenses, and the difficulty of achieving precise and repeatable alignment of lens-to-camera mechanical linkages.

Among 35 mm SLR cameras, nearly all of which offer lens interchangeability, no two manufacturers of bayonet-mount systems share a common, compatible mount. Older, screw-mount SLR's, however, nearly all have a common mount thread, so one manufacturer's lenses may often be used satisfactorily on another manufacturer's camera body.

A third method of achieving lens interchangeability is associated almost exclusively with large-format sheet-film cameras. Each lens is mounted in a square *lens board*, which is secured by clips in a recess in the camera's front lens standard. Lens changes are very fast and easy to perform, as they seldom require more than opening one or two sliding latches, lifting the lens-and-board assembly off the camera, fitting the replacement,

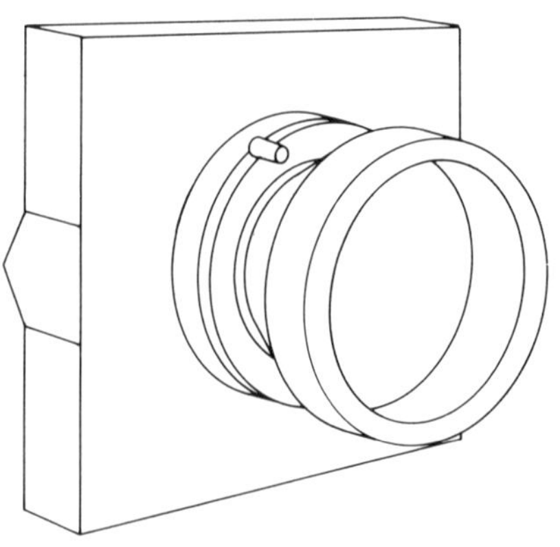

View-camera lenses are generally mounted in lens boards. Board-plus-lens interchanges as unit. Camera's lens standard is recessed for board, which latches in place. System is strong, simple, and convenient.

and relocking the latches. Some standardization of lens-board sizes exists, and adapters are also available for mounting small lens boards in standards recessed for larger boards. In any case, it does not normally require mechanical genius or a professional workshop to make a lens board if and when a special size is needed.

INTERCHANGEABLE ACCESSORY LENSES

Interchangeable accessory lenses may be categorized as follows: fisheye, extreme wide-angle, wide-angle, telephoto, extreme telephoto, zoom, macro, and repro or process lenses. Not all of these lens types are available for all cameras that accept interchangeable lenses, but many usually are. Since 35 mm SLR cameras often accept or can be adapted to accept all of the preceding types, we'll discuss them in relationship to the 35 mm format, bearing in mind that similar uses and effects are involved when a similar lens type is used with a larger-format or smaller-format camera.

WIDE-ANGLE LENSES

Among fisheye, extreme wide-angle, and wide-angle lenses, all of which have focal lengths shorter than that of a normal lens as well as broader fields of view, the moderate wide-angles are the most generally useful. These lenses, with focal lengths ranging from about 24 to 35 mm, strike a reasonable balance between breadth of vision and ease of use. They allow more of the scene to fit into the frame than the normal lens, and they do not exact a penalty of abnormal appearance when used with care. With a moderate wide-angle lens, perspective exaggeration may be largely avoided or deliberately induced quite easily. This is less true of the more extreme wide-angles, with focal lengths ranging from as short as about 15 mm to 21 mm or so. These lenses produce such small images of individual scene elements that for most subjects other than sweeping panoramas they force you to approach quite close to fill the frame with the subject adequately. This enforced proximity virtually assures exaggerated perspective. Depending on the photographer's skill, the pronounced effects associated with extreme wide-angle lenses may be strikingly bold or vulgar and grotesque. Moderate wide-angles are less demanding of the photographer, and are therefore better candidates for a first wide-angle.

Both wide-angle and extreme wide-angle lenses are designed to cover the entire film frame with a rectilinear image. A rectilinear image is one in which the straight lines of the subject are rendered as straight lines on film, right angles in the

Wide-angle lenses exaggerate perspective, rendering nearby scene elements disproportionately large, distant elements disproportionately small. The wider the lens, the more pronounced the effect. Here a 21 mm lens was used.

subject are right angles on film, and curved portions of the subject are represented by similarly curved contours on film. Indeed, rectilinearity is a highly prized characteristic of nearly all photographic lenses. Fisheye lenses are a notable exception.

FISHEYE LENSES

Fisheye lenses come in two basic forms, full-frame and circular-image models. *Full-frame* fisheyes, as the name indicates, produce an image that completely fills the film frame. *Circular-image* fisheyes produce a circular picture that fits within the film format, and is surrounded by unexposed film. Both types produce distinctive curvilinear rendering of straight lines. This delivers an attention-getting visual kick that is frequently not supported by the picture content. Circular-image fisheyes were originally introduced for scientific and technical applications that included recording the entire overhead bowl of the sky. Because of their unique images, they rapidly became fashionable with commercial and journalistic photographers as a means of jazzing up assignments.

Circular-image fisheyes for 35 mm SLR's range in focal length from about 6 to 8.5 mm, and generally cover a field of approximately 180°. One extraordinary fisheye covers a field of 220°, which means that it actually includes in its coverage scene elements that are slightly behind it.

The full-frame fisheye represents an interesting compromise between the rectilinear extreme wide-angle and the curvilinear circular fisheye. The full-frame fisheye generally has a focal length of about 15 mm or 16 mm and an angular coverage of 180° across the diagonal of the film format. As with the circular fisheye, the full-frame fisheye bows straight lines more and more sharply the farther they are from the center of the field. However, the curvature is never so pronounced as with the circular fisheye because the extreme edges of the field, where maximum curvature occurs, are outside the rectangular film format, which is inscribed in the image circle. As a point of passing interest, a full-frame fisheye designed for use with the 35 mm format may serve as a circular-image fisheye lens if it is adapted to a camera that accepts larger film. In this case, the full image circle produced by the lens fits within the larger frame and creates the larger, full-circle fisheye image.

TELEPHOTO LENSES 85 TO 105 mm

For the 35 mm format, the telephoto range begins with focal lengths of 85 to 105 mm. Lenses in this range are extremely popular for candid and journalistic photography, portraits, and, sometimes, for all-around use in place of a normal lens. They are often not oppressively larger or heavier than a normal lens, and many offer usefully large maximum apertures of *f*/2 or thereabouts, so are easily usable in subdued light levels. As the image size produced at a given distance is about twice or slightly less than twice the image size produced with a normal lens, moderate telephotos are very useful for "tightening up" composition and filling the frame with significant subject detail. Yet they do not provide so much image magnification that the photographer is forced to back off to an inconveniently long distance from the subject. The moderate telephoto is probably the most sensible choice as a first long lens for most nonspecialized photographers.

Moderate telephoto, 90 mm in this case, helps tighten composition without disturbing subject. It also includes enough subject area not to require backing off excessively. It's a happy compromise for many photographers.

The combination of a moderate wide-angle and a moderate telephoto, with or without a normal lens, make an exceptionally useful and versatile optical outfit for handling a wide range of subjects and circumstances very well.

135 mm LENSES

A jump beyond moderate telephotos is the 135 mm focal length, which is the traditional and also the most popular all-around telephoto for 35 mm cameras. The 135 mm telephoto lens provides noticeably greater "reach" than the moderate teles, with approximately 2.5× the magnification of the normal lens. It also produces photographs that exhibit slightly compressed, or flattened, perspective, and allows the photographer to keep relatively far from the subject while recording a usefully large image on film.

From the standpoint of handling, 135 mm lenses tend to be larger and heavier than moderate telephoto lenses, and require more care on the part of the photographer. Because of their greater magnification, they render more noticeable blur caused by camera or subject motion, so require the use of higher shutter speeds and steadier support than shorter lenses. Maximum apertures range from about *f*/2 to *f*/4, and most 135 mm lenses focus down to five feet. Although many photographers use the 135 mm focal length for portraits, some are not enthusiastic about the greater working distance the longer lens requires, as they feel it diminishes rapport with the subject. And some photographers feel that the mild telephoto compression the 135 mm lens produces sometimes makes the face in a portrait look slightly flatter than desired.

One limitation of the 135 mm lens relative to the shorter moderate teles should be considered by budget-conscious photographers. The 135 mm lens is simply too much of a telephoto to be used as an all-around lens in place of a normal lens, as can be done with the moderate teles in the 85 to 105 mm range. If you are considering your first telephoto, you should definitely try out both a 135 mm telephoto and a shorter one to determine which has the better visual feel for you.

180 TO 200 mm LENSES

Pronounced depth compression in the photograph and substantial image magnification come into play with focal lengths of 180 mm and 200 mm. The 180's and 200's are the longest lenses that most photographers can use hand-held. Image magnification is approximately 3.5× to 4× that of the normal lens, which permits filling the frame with subjects that are quite distant. Maximum apertures of lenses in this category are normally about

$f/3.5$ to $f/4.5$, but some manufacturers produce $f/2.8$ models at a considerable penalty in size, weight, and price. Theatrical photographers, sports photographers, and photojournalists, who often must capture action at great distances under dim lighting, find such lenses invaluable. Minimum focusing distance of lenses in this category is about eight feet, with occasional exceptions.

Because of the considerable image magnification with 180 mm and 200 mm lenses, steady holding is essential to prevent blur from camera movement, and the use of high shutter speeds such as 1/250 sec. and faster is desirable. Unfortunately, photographers are often overly optimistic about their ability to hold long lenses steady during longish exposures, and the result is fuzzy pictures and allegations of deficient optical quality. If you intend doing much long-lens photography, it will be worth your time and effort at the outset to shoot a series of photographs of a highly detailed subject at various shutter speeds to determine the lowest speed at which you can reliably obtain sharp pictures with the lens in question. If subjects you intend photographing lend themselves to a deliberate, unhurried approach, consider using a sturdy tripod rather than hand-holding the camera.

Aside from the prosaic aspect of using long lenses to bridge distances between camera and subject, the long telephotos have several characteristics that lend themselves well to making

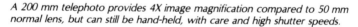

A 200 mm telephoto provides 4X image magnification compared to 50 mm normal lens, but can still be hand-held, with care and high shutter speeds.

Long telephoto lenses produce characteristic compression of foreground and background, flattening perspective. Here, bridge in background is full mile from camera, yet doesn't look much farther than first lamp post, which is only quarter of a mile from camera position. A 400 mm lens pulled them together.

dramatic photographs. Their tendency to flatten out perspective and "mash" foreground, middle ground, and background together into what appears to be almost the same plane may be used to create very graphic, "designy" pictures with a poster-like quality. The relatively great magnification they provide makes it possible to rivet the viewer's gaze powerfully on a subject. And the comparatively shallow depth of field that results from increased image magnification can create dramatically abrupt transitions from the sharply focused plane to softly blurred nearer and farther zones.

300 mm TO 2000 mm LENSES

Most major lens systems for 35 mm SLR cameras offer extreme telephotos with focal lengths ranging up to 1000 mm or even 2000 mm. The progression of focal lengths includes: 300 mm, 400 mm, 500 mm, 600 mm, 800 mm, 1000 mm, 1200 mm, 1600 mm, and 2000 mm. No lens line is likely to comprise all of these focal lengths, as 100 mm more or less do not make an earthshaking difference as one approaches the 1000 mm mark. And some lens systems include odd focal lengths such as 560 mm or 640 mm. As a rule to which there are few exceptions, increases in focal length mean increases in lens length, diameter, weight, cost, and need for rigid support, coupled with decreases in lens speed and general utility.

CATADIOPTRIC LENSES

One subcategory of extreme telephotos deserves special mention because it represents an interesting solution to the problems of excess bulk and weight that afflict conventional designs. Catadioptric, or mirror, telephotos available from a number of manufacturers are uniformly much shorter and lighter than their focal lengths would seem to permit. This is because a system of mirrors within the lens barrel creates a complex folded light path that permits a shorter overall length. For example, one 1600 mm catadioptric lens has an actual length of 12.9 inches. Since 1600 mm is equivalent to almost 63 inches, the size reduction that is possible through catadioptric design is obviously quite dramatic.

Catadioptric lenses, however, bring their own set of special problems. They generally have somewhat slower apertures than conventionally designed lenses of the same focal length, they are somewhat more susceptible to being knocked out of optical alignment by rough handling, and they have nonadjustable apertures. The latter aspect means that the photographer cannot increase depth of field by stopping the lens down. But, for the photographer who shoots many location assignments that require the use of extreme telephoto lenses, the conveniences of

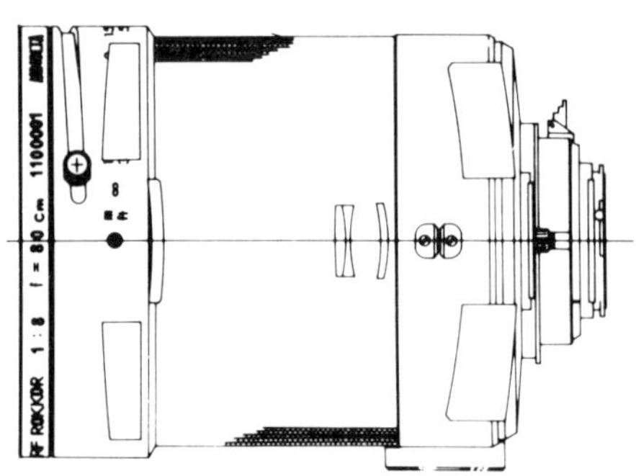

Catadioptric, mirror-type telephotos use mirrors to "fold" light path inside lens. The 800 mm Minolta mirror lens shown has 8 elements, of which 2 are mirrors. Although focal length is 800 mm, actual physical length is only 166 mm. Courtesy Minolta Corporation.

catadioptric design are often more significant than the drawbacks.

As soon as a photographer accumulates enough interchangeable lenses to feel well equipped, he will also begin to notice that they are too heavy to carry around all the time and that the best picture opportunities seem to occur while he is changing lenses. The next step, then, is to seek one lens that will perform the functions of several. The zoom lens is an attempt to satisfy this demand.

ZOOM LENSES

A zoom lens has a variable focal length that may be adjusted continuously from its shortest setting to its longest setting by moving a control on the lens. The relationship between the shortest focal length setting and the longest is called the zoom ratio. Zoom lenses are available in the wide-angle range, from moderate wide-angle to moderate telephoto, and from normal focal length or moderate telephoto to long or even extreme telephoto. And increasingly, zoom lenses are being made with an additional control that permits shifting the lens into a close-focusing mode. The combinations and permutations of zoom lens ranges, maximum apertures, and focusing distances almost defy synopsis. As a starting point in discussing zooms, though, it should be noted that the term zoom lens is used rather loosely in many photographic publications, including this book, to categorize two rather different lens types. The true zoom lens is designed so that changing the focal length does not shift the lens' focus. The other member of the zoom family, which is more properly referred to as a variable-focal-length lens, will shift focus when the focal length setting is changed. From an operational standpoint, the true zoom is faster and more convenient to use because it does not require refocusing with each alteration in focal length. Variable-focal-length lenses, on the other hand, may make up for the need to refocus often by being a bit more compact, or offering a wider maximum aperture, closer focusing, or a slightly lower price, or some appropriate combination of these attributes.

Although it is tempting to regard a zoom lens as a weight-saving, space-saving substitute for two or three or more fixed-focal-length lenses, to do so is to court disappointment and to do the zoom an injustice. The fact is that a zoom lens is nearly always substantially larger and heavier than any one of the lenses it replaces, so the weight you hold to your eye while photographing will be greater with the zoom, although the total weight you carry may be reduced. If you use a tripod often, it won't matter. If you shoot with the camera hand-held for hours at a time, you may find the zoom more fatiguing than a lighter lens on the camera plus two more stuck in your pockets or a camera bag. The real strength and undeniable appeal of the zoom lies in the instant accessibility of a range of focal lengths. This may be extremely important to a sports photographer, for example, who wants to photograph an entire section of the playing field one moment and "zero in" on a particular athlete the next. And this facility is appreciated by photographers who shoot mainly on color transparency films. It lets them fill the frame with precisely the subject matter desired without having to trot back and forth with fixed-focal-length lenses until the right combination of focal length and distance is found.

Traditionally, purists have reproached zoom lenses for being less sharp and contrasty than good fixed-focal-length lenses. Currently, the best zoom lenses from major manufacturers are less vulnerable to this charge than earlier zooms, and can produce images that require no apology.

As a rule, zooms have smaller maximum apertures than the fixed-focal-length lenses they replace, so they are not ideal choices for low-light photography. And close-focus models excepted, they generally do not focus as close, either. Whether or not these factors are drawbacks depends on the type of photography you do, rather than on any absolute guidelines. As for the close-up focusing range built into more and more zooms, which is often described loosely as a "macro" setting, only you can decide whether or not your photographic style justifies the additional expense the feature normally entails. In any case, a zoom lens with close-up capability is not a serious rival in terms of image magnification or optical quality to a true macro lens specially corrected to produce optimum quality at close focusing distances.

MACRO LENSES

Macro lenses for 35 mm SLR's are designed specifically to produce exceptional image quality in close-up photography, and to focus close enough to produce a life-size or nearly life-size image on film. A life-size image is one that is the same size as the subject. To permit continuous focusing from infinity to the minimum focusing distance, macro lenses are built with focusing mounts that allow the lens elements to be moved considerably farther away from the film than would be the case with a conventional lens of similar focal length. Consequently, macro lenses tend to be a bit larger and heavier than their focal lengths

For maximum image quality in close-up photography, it's desirable to use optics such as macro lenses, which are designed for optimum performance at close focusing distances. Fine optics and a very sharp, fine-grain film recorded surface detail of this commemorative medallion.

and maximum apertures would seem to warrant because of the need to accommodate an oversize focusing mechanism.

Macro lenses are most commonly offered in 50 mm and 55 mm normal focal lengths and about 90 to 100 mm moderate telephoto lengths. Maximum apertures range from *f*/2.8 through *f*/4. Larger apertures are not very practical for macro lenses because of the difficulty of correcting the larger lens elements that would be required and the considerable increase in size and weight of the focusing mount that larger elements would demand.

If your interests lean to close-up work, a good macro lens can be an excellent investment, as it will make your photography much easier. Macro lenses are far more convenient for close-up work than alternatives such as extension tubes or bellows units, are self-contained for the most part and therefore easier to carry, and require little if any set-up effort beyond mounting on the camera as with any other lens. And since they focus to infinity, too, they can double as general-purpose normal or short tele lenses, depending on focal length, providing your nonclose-up work does not demand high-speed lenses and providing you don't mind carrying the slightly larger and heavier macro lens.

To help choose between normal and telephoto macro lenses, consider the following points: The short lens, which will allow you to work very close to the subject, is handy for photographing medium-size subjects in confined areas and is very convenient for copying documents or other flat work. The short macro is less convenient for shooting tight close-ups of three-dimensional subjects because the short lens-to-subject distance may create undesirable perspective exaggeration. In studio situations, the working distance with a short macro may be too close to allow sufficient flexibility in positioning lights because of shadows cast by the camera and lens. With the longer-focal-length macro lenses, you have about double the lens-to-subject distance for any given image size, and thus have considerably more freedom to position lights where you want them. On the other hand, the longer distance can sometimes make it awkward or impossible to reach the subject and move it about while observing the effects through the camera.

Note that many macro lenses must be used with an accessory extension ring or tube, sometimes called a life-size adapter, to achieve maximum image size on film. This extension tube fits between the camera body and the lens and lengthens the lens barrel enough to provide the additional magnification needed. The advantage of the life-size adapter system is that the macro lens focusing mount can be made smaller and lighter than if the additional length were to be built in. Also the adapter is often usable with other lenses to extend their focusing range.

REPROGRAPHIC LENSES

For close-up performance that surpasses even that of macro lenses, photographers may turn to *reprographic process*, or *repro*, lenses. Although repro lenses are usually associated with large formats, some are available in shorter focal lengths suitable for 35 mm SLR use. They are very highly corrected for color and sharpness in a focusing range from about one-tenth life-size to life-size. Repro lenses are sometimes used by photographers for critical copying, and in larger formats, for very exacting still-life work. Most repro lenses have modest maximum apertures ranging from about *f*/8 to *f*/16 depending on focal length, the longer lenses usually being slower. What they lack at the large end of the aperture range they sometimes make up for at the small end, though, with minimum apertures in the range of *f*/64 and smaller. These lenses are principally special-purpose optics with limited but useful applicability to conventional photography.

Although the types of lenses discussed in the preceding pages have been related to 35 mm SLR cameras, for all but the most extreme types, equivalents exist for larger-format interchangeable-lens cameras. But what about the photographer who would like to make wide-angle and telephoto shots and close-ups with a camera that does not have interchangeable lenses?

AUXILIARY COMPONENTS AND LENSES

At various times cameras have been produced with a limited capability for lens changing based on a system of auxiliary lens components. In some cases, the front of the normal lens unscrews and is replaced by a wide-angle or telephoto component that works in conjunction with the permanently installed rear elements. Other approaches involve screwing wide-angle or telephoto conversion units on top of the existing normal lens. Both approaches look better on paper than in reality. These systems are limited in the degree of wide-angle and telephoto effects produced, image quality is seldom better than mediocre, and maximum lens speed tends to be less than desirable. The positive side of this generally gloomy picture is that the cameras afflicted with these systems are seldom very high-priced, and the interchangeable components are frequently less expensive than conventional interchangeable lenses.

In the close-up area, relatively inexpensive auxiliary, or supplementary, screw-in lenses may be used with nearly any camera lens in the medium wide-angle, normal, or medium telephoto ranges. Close-up auxiliary lenses come in a variety of strengths, and may be of simple single-element design or more highly corrected multiple-element construction. Both types look similar, so you have to rely on manufacturers' specifications for construction information. They are produced by camera manufacturers as well as by independent optical companies. The most satisfactory image quality is likely to be produced by auxiliary lenses of multiple-element design produced by a camera company specifically for use with one or more of its own lenses. In this instance, the auxiliary lens will have been formulated to match the characteristics of the lens or lenses with which its use is recommended.

The major advantages of auxiliary close-up lenses are that they are economical, small and light, and easy to use. Disadvantages are that they require stopping the prime lens down to fairly small apertures for best results, seldom produce quality equal to that obtainable with a good macro lens, and are restricted to narrow ranges of magnification.

Ironically, auxiliary lenses are most convenient to use with SLR cameras, which need them least, because SLR viewing and focusing are most convenient for close-up photography. When auxiliary lenses are used with cameras that do not have through-the-lens viewing and focusing, focus must be established with reference to tables supplied with the auxiliary lens, relating distance setting on the camera lens to the actual working distance with the auxiliary lens and the size of the subject field produced. Precise composition is out of the question, but with experience, serviceable results may be achieved.

Similar criticisms may be made regarding the use of wide-angle and telephoto conversion components on cameras lacking SLR finders, although separate optical viewfinders may be available for mounting on the camera to indicate wide-angle and tele fields of view. They are less convenient to use than the camera's basic finder system, but with moderate to far away subjects, compositional discrepancies will seldom be objectionable.

LENS COATING

Nearly all photographic lenses consist of more than one optical element. The more elaborate the design, the more elements end up in the lens barrel. Although we think of lens elements as transmitting light, the fact is that a lens does not transmit to the film in coherent image form all the light that initially enters the optical system. A certain amount is lost along the way, with some of the most serious losses occurring at interfaces between glass surfaces and air. The highly polished lens surfaces bounce small but significant quantities of light out of the desired optical path. Such light may ricochet randomly within the lens, bounce off the diaphragm blades and interior of the lens barrel, and only then end up at the film as nonimage-forming light. Some of the diverted light will not reach the film at all.

Scattering and bouncing of light within a photographic lens is undesirable because nonimage-forming light that reaches the film degrades picture quality. It may do so dramatically, as a bright, repeating pattern of reflections that more or less obscure the desired image. It may do so more subtly, producing a veiled, foglike, contrast-reducing haze over the negative or transparency. Although these effects have been used deliberately to create photographs of great beauty, when they occur spontaneously and unpredictably they are generally ruinous. Therefore, optical companies have expended vast amounts of research time and funds on efforts to subdue light scattering and internal reflections in camera lenses.

Shortly before World War II, a major breakthrough

occurred in the form of lens coating. Microscopically fine layers of certain chemical compounds deposited on the surface of lens elements in a vacuum chamber formed effective antireflection coatings that markedly reduced light scattering and dispersion. Camera lenses incorporating this technique are called coated lenses. By the early postwar period, nearly all high-quality photographic lenses were coated.

Then lens designers began producing increasingly complex lenses to satisfy demands for higher lens speeds, wider angles of view, and zoom lenses. The number of elements in lenses began going up, the size of the elements often increased, and the curvature of the surfaces tended to become more extreme. All of which encouraged the generation of internal reflections and scattering.

To combat these problems, by the early 1970's multiple-layer lens coating surfaced. Multiple-layer coating is exactly what the name implies. Instead of coating a lens surface with one layer of antireflection material, 3, 5, 7, 9, 11, or more layers of various antireflection coating may be deposited.

Multiple-layer lens coating can be extremely effective in reducing lens flare and internal reflections when it is used appropriately. The key word is appropriately. Multiple-coating a poorly designed lens will not magically make it outstanding. In short, multiple-layer lens coating is a valid and useful technique when it is used selectively and intelligently. But it is not a cure-all and its presence does not guarantee that a lens will necessarily outperform or even match the quality of a high-quality, conventionally coated lens of the same general type.

Multiple-layer coating is used most often on lenses for interchangeable-lens 35 mm and roll-film cameras, particularly with extreme wide-angle and zoom designs that are inherently very vulnerable to internal reflections and flare. Multiple coating has made fewer inroads with lenses for large-format cameras, although it probably will eventually. The rationale appears to be that the smaller cameras are more likely to be used under essentially uncontrolled lighting conditions, while the larger cameras are generally used with carefully adjusted studio lighting or preplanned natural lighting.

On a practical level, if you are about to invest in a new camera outfit, or additional new lenses for a camera system you already have, you will probably not have to choose between multiple coating and conventional coating. The manufacturer of the lens will have made the choice for you. With older used lenses, you may find both conventionally coated and multiple-coated models for the same cameras. The later, multiple-coated lenses are generally preferable, unless the price differential is unacceptably great or it is known that the earlier versions were demonstrably superior.

If you haven't decided which camera system you will purchase, do not overemphasize lens coating techniques as a determinant. The handling qualities of the cameras you're considering, the ease and accuracy with which you can focus them, the accessories available, and their applicability to your photographic interests are all more important in the long run than how many layers of what materials were deposited on which lens surfaces. You may find that one manufacturer's line of conventionally coated lenses generally outperforms another manufacturer's line of multiple-coated lenses. You may also discover that a number of competing lens systems of approximately equal price levels offer practically indistinguishable performance.

LENS SPEED

An area of choice that is more significant to the photographer about to buy one or more lenses concerns maximum aperture of the lenses. Particularly in 35 mm systems, a manufacturer may offer two or more lenses of differing maximum aperture in the same focal length. With normal lenses, for example, you may have a choice of apertures including an expensive super-fast, *f*/1.2 lens, a less expensive high-speed *f*/1.4 model, and a comparatively economical lens with a maximum aperture in the range of *f*/1.7 to *f*/2. Which should you buy? It's a simple question, but not one that can be answered very simply. Ultimately, you will have to weigh factors of cost, convenience, size, and weight to come up with an answer that will make sense for you. A professional photojournalist who often has to get his picture in poor light or not at all might choose the fastest lenses available, even though they will be larger, heavier, and more expensive than the slower alternatives. An amateur photographer who concentrates on outdoor subjects in generally good weather might well be content with medium-speed or slower lenses that are more than fast enough for outdoor daylight situations. They cost less and are easier to carry because they are smaller and lighter. A sports photographer may prefer a 200 mm *f*/2.8 telephoto that lets him shoot at high, action-stopping shutter speeds even in dim light, and a backpacker might be happier with an *f*/4.5 version that weighs half or two-thirds as much. A photographer who uses SLR cameras may find it difficult to focus easily with slower lenses because of the relative dimness of the image on the ground glass. A photographer using a rangefinder camera can focus fast or slow lenses with equal ease, since the focusing system is optically separate from the taking lens. Analyzing your own specific needs and preferences will provide a good basis on which to decide about which lenses will be most useful in fast versions and which in slower models.

If you are considering buying used lenses dating from the 1960's or earlier, you may obtain better optical performance from moderate-speed models than from the fastest versions. With high-quality lenses of recent design, medium-speed and high-speed models are likely to offer equal image quality.

SPECIAL-PURPOSE LENSES

PERSPECTIVE-CORRECTION LENSES

Besides the major types of lenses already discussed, several special-purpose designs are worth noting. For users of 35 mm SLR's who are particularly interested in architecture, so-called perspective-correction, or PC, lenses allow photographing buildings without making them look as though they were tilted backward or converging to a needle point. PC lenses do this by combining a wide-angle field of view with an oversized image circle and a complex mount that permits shifting the lens vertically and/or horizontally relative to the mounting flange. By shifting the lens up, the photographer can include the top of a building in a picture without having to tilt the camera up. Thus the film plane in the camera can remain parallel with the vertical axis of the building, and the vertical lines of the subject will be parallel on film. The oversized image circle the PC lens produces provides the covering power necessary to fill the film frame with a good-quality image even when the lens is shifted appreciably off center. Most shift lenses for 35 mm SLR's are 35 mm wide-angles with maximum apertures in the *f*/2.8 to *f*/4 range. Although they can double as general-purpose wide-angle lenses in a pinch, most PC lenses do not offer the convenience of automatic diaphragm operation, and they tend to be larger and heavier than conventional designs, as well as more expensive.

VARIABLE-FIELD-CURVATURE LENSES

In 1974, Minolta Camera Co., Ltd., introduced a unique 24 mm *f*/2.8 wide-angle lens with a special control permitting the photographer to adjust the lens' field of sharp focus continuously from convex through flat to concave. This VFC (variable-field-curvature) lens thus can tailor its field of focus to conform to variously curved subject contours or arrangements to maximize sharpness even when depth of field alone is inadequate to cover important areas. Conversely, the VFC feature may also be used to decrease sharpness selectively. Since the lens is about the same size and weight as a conventional 24 mm *f*/2.8 wide-angle, it serves nicely as a general-purpose lens when the VFC control is in its neutral, flat-field setting. In 1976, Minolta one-upped their 24 mm VFC lens by introducing a 35 mm *f*/2.8 PC-type lens that also provides variable-field-curvature control and was alone at the time among PC lenses in having an automatic diaphragm. This is an exceptionally ingenious lens that offers the 35 mm photographer previously unattainable image-management options, but it is definitely large, heavy, and very expensive.

SOFT-FOCUS OR PORTRAIT LENSES

For photographers specializing in portraiture, soft-focus or portrait lenses are available. They are designed to form flatteringly diffuse, pearly images that subdue skin texture and minor complexion flaws that would otherwise be cruelly apparent. Such lenses provide a form of instant retouching at the moment the film is exposed. Most portrait lenses tend to produce very diffuse images at wide apertures, and increasingly sharp images as they are stopped down to small apertures. This allows the photographer to control the degree of diffusion according to subject requirements and preferences. Because of changing tastes in portraiture, relatively few true portrait lenses are still produced, but they are often available "used." Most are in focal lengths equivalent to moderate telephoto for the respective film format, as it is assumed that they will be used to fill the frame with a head-and-shoulders image. Maximum apertures are generally moderate, presupposing the availability of adequate studio lighting. Portrait lenses designed for 35 mm cameras are rare, probably because the primary thrust of lens development for this format has been toward greater rather than lesser sharpness. Most photographers currently work on the reasonable assumption that they can always drape gauze over a sharp lens to produce a romantically soft image on occasion, but there is no way to make critically sharp images with a soft-focus lens.

INDEPENDENT MANUFACTURERS' LENSES

A question often posed by people about to buy accessory lenses concerns the relative merits of independent manufacturers' lens lines versus the camera manufacturers' lens systems. Stripped to essentials, the question usually means: Does it make sense for me to put an inexpensive lens on an expensive camera? In a word, the answer is maybe.

In recent years, manufacturers of high-quality 35 mm cameras have observed with horror the rapid growth of independent lens manufacturers and marketing organizations. Their horror stems from the unpleasant fact that nearly all have lost considerable accessory lens sales to the independents. The reasons the independents are flourishing are simple enough. Their lenses are usually less expensive than the original-equipment-manufacturer's equivalents, and in some cases the independents provide lenses that are more innovative or versatile than a camera manufacturer's offerings.

BRAND LENS OR INDEPENDENT

Deciding whether to stick to camera-brand lenses or go the independent route varies according to circumstances. If you have the money to spend, by all means buy lenses made by the manufacturer of your camera bodies if they come in the right apertures, focal lengths, and types to suit your purposes. There is no denying that the manufacturers of high-quality cameras are under considerable pressure to maintain correspondingly high standards of lens design, production, and inspection. From the standpoint of safeguarding their reputations and positions in a highly competitive market, they cannot afford to do less.

If economy is a serious factor for you, consider buying camera-brand lenses for the focal lengths you will be using heavily, and independent brands for the lenses you will be using less frequently. It's more than likely that a good brand of independent lens will be as robust as the camera-brand equivalent, but if it isn't, the difference will probably not be apparent if the lens isn't used on an almost daily basis. And of course, if a lens you need exists only in an independently made version, you may as well go ahead, since you have no other alternative.

One last caution regarding independent versus camera-brand lenses is to compare prices carefully. List prices of nearly all photographic equipment bear absurdly little relationship to actual selling prices because of prevalent deep discounting. If you shop around, you may discover that the independent lens you planned to buy for the sake of economy might end up costing a few dollars more than the "high-priced" camera-brand lens. This may happen when a dealer suddenly realizes he's overstocked on certain lenses and sells them at barely above cost because he needs the storage space or more working capital, or he bought a ton cheaply through a special promotion, or the distributor/manufacturer panicked and initiated a "rebate" program. If you shop carefully and are not in a hurry to buy, you may be able to find the camera-brand lens at a lower price than you thought possible.

6

Exposure Control

To produce a technically acceptable picture, the film in the camera must be exposed to image-forming light long enough to record subject form, detail, and tonal relationships in a plausible way. If the film is not exposed sufficiently, as in underexposure, it will record too little information regarding the subject's texture, shape, and tone. Severely underexposed negative films will look clear and transparent, reversal films will be black and opaque. Film that is overexposed will not yield useful information about the subject either, when the exposure level rises beyond acceptable limits. Severely overexposed negative films will be densely black, and reversal films may be "burned out" and become transparent. Proper exposure in a given situation requires achieving a balance between film sensitivity, or film speed, and the brightness of the light reflected from the subject toward the camera, which is a function both of the overall illumination level and the tone and reflective characteristics of the subject.

With simple, nonadjustable snapshot cameras, the photographer can control exposure only to the extent that he can choose a film of appropriate sensitivity for the expected lighting conditions, then take pictures when the light is right and refrain from taking pictures when the light becomes too bright or too dim. Most snapshot cameras are preset at the factory with a fixed shutter speed and lens aperture suitable for shooting with medium-speed films of ASA 64 through ASA 125 under fairly bright outdoor conditions. Good results may also be obtained as the light diminishes to levels encountered under moderate overcast. This broad range of acceptable lighting conditions works because the medium-speed films generally exhibit good exposure latitude, or tolerance for moderate under- and overexposure. The same fixed exposure settings are also satisfactory for indoor photography with recommended flash sources over a limited but useful range of flash-to-subject distances normally specified in the owner's manual that accompanies the camera. Theoretically, only one distance is correct for a given flash intensity, but again, film latitude provides a useful cushion to fall back on.

Cameras with adjustable shutter speeds and lens apertures provide vastly greater flexibility with regard to exposure control, and are capable of making properly exposed photographs under a very wide range of lighting conditions. By increasing or decreasing the shutter speed and opening or closing the lens diaphragm, the photographer can regulate the amount of light that reaches the film. To do so effectively, though, he must know how bright the light illuminating the subject is, or how much light the subject is reflecting toward the camera. And he must be able to relate this information to the speed of the film in terms of the shutter speed and *f*-stop required to produce proper exposure.

Because the human eye is a notoriously poor judge of light levels for photographic purposes, most photographers use a *light meter*, or *exposure meter*. An exposure meter is a light-sensitive instrument designed to measure the amount of light reflected toward the camera from the subject (reflected-light meter) or the intensity of light illuminating the subject (incident-light meter). The photographer presets the meter for the ASA speed of the film, makes a light reading, and is rewarded with a quantification

Reflected-light meter measures brightness of light reflected from subject toward camera. Meter may be aimed at subject from camera or closer position, but should face along lens axis in either case.

of the light, presented in terms of shutter and lens settings required to achieve proper exposure. He then can set the camera lens and shutter accordingly.

HAND-HELD METERS

Hand-held exposure meters may be classified according to the types of sensing cells they employ and the manner in which they are used. Photoelectric meters are so named because the sensing cell, usually *selenium*, generates a small but measurable electric current when it is exposed to light. The stronger the light, the stronger the current. The current is fed to a meter movement that deflects an indicator needle on a calibrated scale to provide a usable reading. Selenium-cell meters react quickly to changes in light levels, are accurate with various light sources and do not require batteries to function. They do not, however, lend themselves to miniaturization because selenium cells have to be fairly large to work efficiently, they are not sensitive enough to work in very dim light, and the meter movements are fragile and susceptible to shock damage.

The other major class of exposure meter uses sensing cells that are *photoresistors*. The first great wave of photoresistor-type meters had cadmium sulfide (CdS) light-sensing cells, and the CdS cell remains popular for meters. Unlike selenium, CdS and other photoresistors do not generate an electric current when exposed to light. Instead, they vary their resistance to the passage of electricity as the intensity of light to which they are exposed increases or decreases. All photoresistor-type exposure meters

Incident-light meter measures intensity of light illuminating subject. It is normally held near subject, with receptor aimed toward camera. Any position that lights receptor like subject while facing camera will do.

require one or more batteries to provide a relatively stable supply of electrical energy. When making a light reading, the meter attempts to pass a flow of current across the photoresistor. A meter movement, light-emitting diodes (LED's), or other form of display tells the photographer how much current the photoresistor is passing, which indicates how much light is affecting it. This information is presented in terms of suitable photographic exposure data.

Besides CdS, silicon (Si) and gallium-arsenic-phosphorus (GAP) cells are used in photoresistor-type metering systems. All three offer excellent low-light sensitivity and can be employed in small metering systems. Both Si and GAP cells respond faster than CdS, and are less susceptible to being "dazzled" by exposure to very bright light. CdS cells that have been inadvertently exposed to intensely bright light may give inaccurate readings for minutes or even hours after such exposure. The major disadvantage of the photoresistors is that they are totally dependent on battery power. Dead batteries mean a dead meter, at least until the battery or batteries can be replaced. Reliance on batteries also implies possible problems in cold weather at freezing or lower temperatures, as cold-soaked batteries temporarily lose their ability to deliver rated power. These drawbacks notwithstanding, photoresistors are well suited for use in miniaturized, built-in metering systems.

Both photoelectric and photoresistor-type light meters are available in two predominant styles for measuring either *reflected light* or *incident light.* Reflected-light meters are aimed toward the subject in line with the taking lens of the camera. The object is to ascertain the amount of light reflected from the subject toward the camera. Incident-light meters are held as close to the subject as possible and aimed toward the camera position, to determine the intensity of the light illuminating the side of the subject that is to be photographed. (Many hand-held exposure meters may be used for reflected and incident readings via built-in or accessory adapters.) Both types work well for photographers who understand how to use them.

BUILT-IN EXPOSURE METERS

The reflected-light meter was the natural choice for incorporation into a camera, because it reads light by looking at the subject more or less from the camera's point of view. Reflected-light meters built into cameras with noninterchangeable lenses are generally designed to read an area that corresponds approximately to the field of view of the camera lens. This reduces the likelihood of the meter reading being affected by an atypically light or dark area outside the area that is actually being photographed. The logical questions arise, "What about cameras with interchangeable lenses? How do you make the built-in meter read correctly with extreme wide-angles, normal lenses, and super-telephotos?"

Early models of interchangeable-lens cameras with built-in meters left the solution of this problem to the photographer. The meter was regulated to read roughly the field of the normal lens, and the owner's manual, if it was a good one, advised the photographer to move near the subject for a close-up reading if he could when working with a long telephoto, then back off to make the picture. If the photographer was using a wide-angle lens, the advice was to back away to make an exposure reading of the broader swath of scenery the lens would see, then move in to the actual shooting distance to make the picture. These working methods did little to make the photographer's life easier, which, after all, was the original reason for building the meter into the camera.

THROUGH-THE-LENS METERS

The breakthrough in effectively matching meter coverage to lens coverage came from Asahi Optical Co., manufacturers of Pentax cameras. They reasoned that the best way to guarantee that the built-in meter would read only what was going to be recorded on film would be to have the meter read through the lens that was actually going to take the photograph. No matter what lens was attached to the camera, the meter would determine the exposure with reference to the image formed by the lens.

Photographers were quick to appreciate the advantages of through-the-lens metering, and so were other manufacturers. Currently, every major manufacturer of interchangeable-lens 35 mm cameras offers some form of through-the-lens exposure control, and this convenience has also spread to the field of roll-film single-lens reflex cameras. Large-format view cameras are not completely left out, as accessory meters that fit the camera back like a film holder are available to provide through-the-lens readings.

Perhaps the most appreciated convenience of through-the-lens exposure control is that the photographer can monitor the light meter and adjust the camera controls as needed while looking through the camera viewfinder. This permits keeping track of moving subjects and changing situations without the

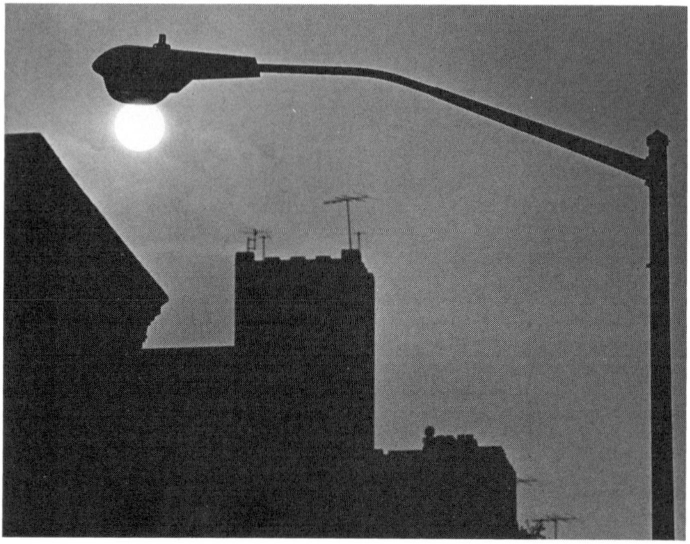

Sun apparently hanging from street lamp was photographed on heavily overcast day that attenuated sun's brightness enough to photograph safely without protective filtration. Exposure reading was made with reflected-light meter, and used as point of departure for deliberate underexposure to dramatize scene.

distraction of putting the camera down periodically to consult a separate instrument every time the light level changes. All through-the-lens metering systems present exposure information in the camera viewfinder in some form that allows the user to adjust the camera at eye level. The simplest displays consist of a moving needle that must be matched to a specific index point by adjusting the lens diaphragm and/or shutter-speed dial. More elaborate displays may include LED indicators and scales that show exactly what shutter speed and *f*-stop have been set. In all cases, the object is to let you make accurate exposures with maximum speed and convenience.

Besides convenience, through-the-lens metering provides the advantage of high potential accuracy no matter what lenses, lens attachments, filters, or diffusion materials the photographer uses. Good through-the-lens meters produce accurate exposure data when used with extreme wide-angle, extreme telephoto and macro lenses, close-up bellows units and extension tubes, or just about any other lens accessory.

Through-the-lens meter systems exist in a variety of configurations, which may be subdivided according to whether readings are made with the lens stopped down to the taking aperture or wide open at maximum aperture, and according to the portion of the image area that is read by the light-sensitive cell or cells: full image area or selective area.

STOPPED-DOWN METERS

The earliest through-the-lens meters made stopped-down readings, which required closing the lens aperture until the meter indicated a proper *f*-stop had been set for the film speed, light level, and preselected shutter speed. If the photographer preferred to shoot at a specific aperture, he would adjust the shutter speed until the meter indicated proper exposure. On a theoretical level, stopped-down readings are potentially more accurate because they take into account whatever discrepancies in light transmission and diaphragm calibration a lens may exhibit. In practice, this system requires additional fiddling with a stop-down lever or button before a valid reading can be made, and the viewfinder image in an SLR becomes progressively dimmer as the lens is stopped down.

Average distribution of light and dark tones and even lighting make this an easy subject to meter accurately with any through-the-lens meter system.

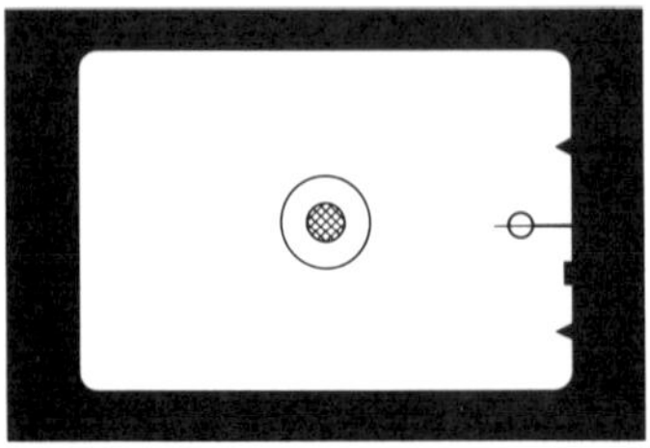

Through-the-lens metering system of Minolta SR-T 200 35 mm SLR permits setting exposure manually at eye level. When meter indicator needle and circle-tipped follower visible in finder are superimposed as shown, exposure is set. Courtesy Minolta Corporation.

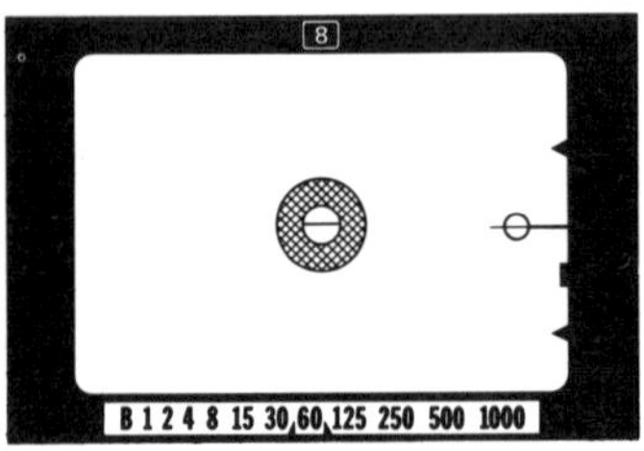

More elaborate finder display of Minolta SR-T 202 35 mm SLR shows aperture to which lens has been set above focusing screen and speed to which shutter has been set on scale below screen. Matching circle-tipped wand to meter needle by adjusting f/stop and/or shutter speed sets exposure. Courtesy Minolta Corporation.

FULL-APERTURE METERS

Full-aperture through-the-lens meters do everything a through-the-lens meter should do, with no need to stop the lens down to make the reading. Lenses designed for use with full-aperture meter systems usually have a special pin or other signalling device incorporated into the mount to "tell" the meter system what the maximum aperture is. The diaphragm setting mechanism also has a signalling device that informs the meter what aperture is being preset. The meter system is designed to reconcile its reading of light at maximum aperture with the mechanically or electrically supplied information that the exposure may be made at some other, smaller aperture. The obvious benefit is that the photographer does not have to lose time stopping the lens down to set the exposure. The primary disadvantage is the greater complexity of the system, which manifests itself in slightly higher cost.

Photographers' preferences for full-aperture metering have been strong enough to drive traditional stopped-down metering from the marketplace. However, several manufacturers use fast-response meter cells to produce stopped-down metering systems that are operated as though they were full-aperture systems. Although they are technically not full-aperture metering systems, they behave as though they were.

Although stopped-down and full-aperture metering have been discussed as separate systems, all full-aperture systems are capable of being used in a stopped-down reading mode at least part of the time. This is necessary to permit accurate metering with lenses that may lack the special coupling pins or aperture-signalling devices required for full-aperture operation, and with close-up equipment such as bellows extension units, which rarely permit full-aperture metering.

If you're contemplating buying new camera equipment with through-the-lens metering, your choice will be among full-aperture systems or stopped-down systems that behave like full-aperture systems. If you're considering used equipment, there are quite a few cameras around that feature stopped-down metering. They are likely to cost less than comparable-quality cameras with full-aperture metering of the same vintage in similar condition. If the uses you have in mind do not require the ultimate in fast exposure setting, a used camera with a stopped-down meter may be just as good. If fast, spontaneous shooting is your passion, though, you will be better off paying a slight premium for the additional convenience of full-aperture exposure control.

INTEGRATED OR AVERAGING METERS

Through-the-lens meter systems may also be differentiated according to how much of the image area they read. Meters that respond to the full image area are said to make *integrated readings*, because they attempt to integrate, or average, all the brightnesses in the scene to come up with a single exposure criterion. Full-area metering is easy to use, because it does not place the burden of choice on the photographer unnecessarily. As long as the scene framed in the viewfinder does not contain abnormally bright or dark irrelevant areas, the exposure data will

Full-area through-the-lens meters average all brightness levels included in field of view. Center-weighted systems base exposure more on brightness levels near center of field and less on inputs from areas toward edges. Spot meters read only clearly defined area within field, and ignore brightness levels elsewhere.

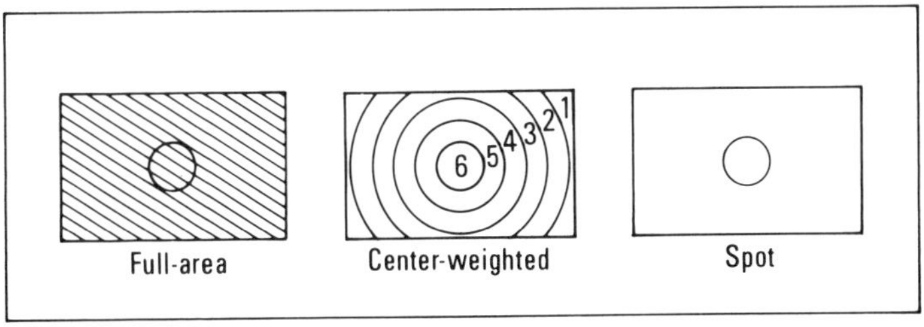

result in technically good pictures nearly all the time. An unusually bright highlight area in the background or foreground, such as a reflection of the sun in a window, however, can throw less brilliant primary subjects into dark underexposure by boosting the average brightness of the total scene as perceived by an integrating meter. The reverse can also occur when an unusually dark extraneous area lowers the average scene brightness enough to cause overexposure of the significant subject area.

That integrating meters can be tricked into erroneous readings by atypical distributions of brightness should not be taken as an invalidation of the concept. It simply means that the photographer using an integrating through-the-lens meter should stay alert to the brightness distribution in the subjects he photographs. Then he can alter the meter's exposure recommendations appropriately when a scene contains irrelevant extremes of light or dark.

SELECTIVE-AREA AND SPOT METERS

Selective-area or spot-through-the-lens meters are designed to read the brightness of a specific part of the scene framed by the viewfinder, rather than the entire area. Typically, the reading area will be indicated by an outline on the focusing screen of the camera, or will at least be diagrammed in the owner's manual. Selective-area meters that read only a very small portion of the image are often described as spot meters.

Selective-area through-the-lens meters require more judgment on the part of the photographer than integrating meters. If the selective-area reading is to provide valid exposure information, it must be aimed at a part of the scene that exhibits representative scene brightness. If the reading zone is superimposed on a part of the scene that is substantially brighter than the rest, everything except the measured area will be underexposed in the picture; or if the reading area is darker than the rest of the scene, the bulk of the picture will be overexposed. The photographer must appraise the scene in terms of light and dark and decide which parts of the scene are appropriate reference points for metering purposes, and then use only those areas for exposure readings. Proponents of selective-area meters claim that the potentially greater accuracy of these systems compensates for the greater care required to use them effectively, but for beginning photographers or for those who are not enthralled by the prospect of thinking more than minimally about exposure determination, selective-area metering can be a chore. However, for special applications, selective-area metering can be excellent. If you often photograph subjects that are substantially lighter or darker than surrounding areas, as is frequently the case in theatrical photography, for example, a spot meter is the most efficient way to peg exposure to an actor's face without worries about odd areas of conflicting tone.

WEIGHTED METERS

In an attempt to give photographers the best of both systems, some manufacturers have gone to so-called weighted through-the-lens exposure meters. Weighted systems normally read the entire image area, but instead of averaging brightness democratically, they emphasize readings in one part of the scene. In a center-weighted system, the meter will be most influenced by brightness perceived in the center of the image area, and will be considerably less affected by light or dark areas near the edges of the field. Not all weighted meter systems emphasize the center, so the owner of a camera with a weighted meter should give some thought to where the emphasis is placed. For example, a center-weighted system might be preferable if you intend to do a great deal of portrait photography. A photographer who is passionately addicted to landscape photography might prefer a bottom-weighted meter that will emphasize the land mass and downplay sky brightness. Of course, either photographer can use either system perfectly well as long as he is aware of its peculiarities, but it's still advantageous to match the system to the application when a happy match can be made.

SWITCHABLE SYSTEMS

A few cameras have appeared that attempt to be all things to all people in terms of exposure measurement. They incorporate two meter systems with a selector switch. One setting provides selective-area or true spot readings, the other provides integrated readings. A switchable exposure system may prove useful to an experienced and disciplined photographer, but for most people, it represents superfluous complexity.

AUTOMATIC EXPOSURE CONTROL

As quick and easy as it is to adjust lens aperture and shutter speed with reference to a built-in or through-the-lens exposure meter, it's even quicker and easier if the meter itself does the adjusting without the photographer's intervention. Consequently, automatic exposure control was developed to make the photographer freer than ever of technical involvement with the photographic process.

Automatic-exposure systems exist in four basic configurations: programmed, shutter-priority, aperture-priority, and dual-mode systems. They all end up setting exposure automatically, but in different ways.

PROGRAMMED EXPOSURE

Programmed automatic-exposure systems are the most numerous, as they are commonly used in noninterchangeable-lens cartridge-loading and 35 mm cameras that are mainstays of the popular-priced snapshot-camera market. They also have been used in a variety of instant-picture cameras. Typically, a programmed automatic system gets information about light levels and film speed from a built-in exposure meter with its cell window in the camera body or at the front of the lens barrel, just beyond the edge of the lens. The latter location is often used with 35 mm cameras because it permits the cell to read through and thus compensate for any filter the photographer mounts on the lens. The only manual input required of the photographer is to set the meter system for the ASA speed of the film in the camera. With cartridge-loading and instant cameras, even that may be unnecessary. According to the brightness levels the meter detects, the meter system will adjust both the camera's shutter speed and lens aperture to produce proper exposure. Many cameras of this type incorporate warning signals in the viewfinder that tell the photographer when the light is too bright or too dim to make a properly exposed picture. The shutter speed and *f*-stop that will be used to take the picture may also be indicated.

The programs selected by camera designers may differ markedly, so it's desirable to find out before purchasing a programmed camera if the manner in which it shifts exposure settings is compatible with the types of pictures you expect to take. For example, a very popular type of exposure program will select the highest shutter speed and smallest lens aperture in very bright light, then progressively slow the shutter *and* widen the aperture as the light level drops, until at very low light levels the slowest shutter speed and widest aperture are brought into play. In contrast, another program may also start off in very bright light with the highest speed and smallest aperture, then open the aperture gradually as the light level drops. This system may not begin to slow the shutter speed until the lens has opened as far as it can. If you intend to photograph much action, which places a premium on using high shutter speeds to stop motion clearly on film, the latter system will do a much better job for you than the former, because the programming will always try to give you the benefit of the highest shutter speed that conditions permit. On the other hand, if your photography runs to scenery more than rapid action, the former system will do a very good job of providing usable shutter-speed/aperture combinations that do not sacrifice depth of field unnecessarily by opening the aperture in preference to slowing the shutter.

There are also programs that combine the two approaches outlined above. They generally open the aperture a bit, then slow the shutter slightly, then open the aperture some more, then slow the shutter again, and so on. If the programming information isn't spelled out clearly in the owner's manual accompanying the camera, you can nearly always get it from the manufacturer or distributor. The important point is to get the information before you get the camera.

Some cameras featuring programmed automatic exposure also allow bypassing the automatic system and setting shutter speeds and lens apertures manually. This is very desirable if you think that you or someone else using the camera will want to go beyond the possibilities of programmed exposure. Among cameras providing optional manual exposure setting, some permit using the built-in exposure meter manually and others lose the metering function when switched off automatic. The former category is preferable unless you already own and know how to use a hand-held light meter. The chief virtue of programmed automatic exposure is that it is easy to use and produces good results most of the time. The chief drawback is that it offers the photographer little or no control over action-stopping or depth of field.

SHUTTER-PRIORITY SYSTEMS

Shutter-priority auto-exposure systems permit the photographer to select a specific shutter speed while the auto-exposure system varies the lens aperture in response to changing light levels. A "distress" signal of sorts is normally incorporated into the viewfinder of the camera to alert the user when the auto-exposure system has run out of *f*-stops and cannot achieve a proper exposure setting at the selected shutter speed. (The automatically set aperture may also be indicated in the finder.) The user can change to a shutter speed that will allow proper exposure at an aperture available on the camera lens, can forego taking the picture, or can take it at the original shutter speed with the knowledge that it will be over- or underexposed. Shutter-priority systems are found both in 35 mm noninterchangeable-lens cameras and, to a more limited extent, in 35 mm single-lens reflex cameras.

The outstanding advantage of shutter-priority automation is that the photographer chooses the shutter speed that will be used to make the exposure, and thus retains full control over the camera's ability to "freeze" action or blur it. This aspect of image control is particularly important to photographers who cover sporting events or other activities that involve considerable subject and camera motion. The drawbacks of shutter-priority systems include mechanical complexity and loss of auto-exposure capability with various close-up accessories as well as lenses not specifically designed for compatibility with the specific exposure system.

APERTURE-PRIORITY SYSTEMS

Aperture-priority systems operate in the reverse of shutter-priority systems. With an aperture-priority camera, you set the desired lens aperture and the camera's auto-exposure system sets whatever shutter speed is required to achieve proper exposure. Because the shutter speed needed to match a given combination of film speed, aperture, and light level may well be an odd fraction that falls between the usual marked values, aperture-priority systems are coupled to electronically governed shutters with continuously variable speeds. Aperture-priority systems are thus able to deliver, in theory at least, accuracy that goes beyond the actual requirements of most photographic situations. As the light level changes, the shutter speed will change, too, and if the speed required for optimum exposure accuracy is an odd one, such as 1/93 sec., that's what the system will command the shutter to provide.

Simpler cameras with aperture priority generally have viewfinder signals to warn the photographer when the shutter cannot set itself to a high or slow enough speed to avoid over- or underexposure. More elaborate aperture-priority cameras also provide a shutter-speed display in the viewfinder to indicate what speed the auto-exposure system is selecting.

The outstanding advantage of aperture-priority auto-exposure systems is versatility. They continue to provide automatic exposure control with any lens you can physically attach to the camera body; with close-up accessories such as bellows units and extension tubes; with microscopes; with telescopes; with any other optical device or gadget. And aperture-priority systems are ideal for use with catadioptric super-telephoto lenses, which lack adjustable diaphragms. The main drawback of aperture-priority automation is that the photographer must monitor shutter speed carefully, or risk an occasional perfectly exposed blur. If the subjects you prefer require carefully controlling the rendition of movement on film, you would be well advised to consider using a manually set camera, a shutter-priority automatic system, or an aperture-priority system with prominent shutter-speed indication, in the order listed. If you like to photograph action and are confident that you can keep your eye on the shutter speed, do not hesitate to try an aperture-priority camera.

DUAL-MODE SYSTEM

The dual-mode auto-exposure system is a logical development to counter the drawbacks inherent in both aperture-priority and shutter-priority auto-exposure systems. It does so by incorporating both forms of automation into one camera, with a selector switch for locking in the operating mode that is most suitable for the subjects at hand. Minolta Camera Co., Ltd., recently introduced the first 35 mm SLR with dual-mode operation to world markets. The following observations are therefore based on the Minolta approach to dual-mode automation, with the expectation that other manufacturers' versions, following Minolta's lead, will solve similar problems in essentially similar ways.

When the dual-mode camera is set for shutter-priority auto-exposure, it can be used only with a series of lenses that incorporate the mechanism required to let the camera change the diaphragm opening. The aperture scales on these lenses have a special setting that signifies camera-guided diaphragm automation. The aperture-setting ring must index at this position for shutter-priority automation. The photographer selects the shutter speed conventionally, and the camera proceeds to adjust the lens aperture as required. The manually set shutter speed and automatically selected lens aperture are displayed in the viewfinder.

For aperture-priority operation, the selector switch must be set to the appropriate marking, and the lens diaphragm ring moved to the desired aperture setting. The camera's electronically timed shutter will now provide continuously variable shutter speeds, and will set itself to whatever speed is required for the film speed, aperture selected, and light level. The viewfinder display indicates the shutter speed that is being automatically set and the lens aperture the user has set manually. In the aperture-priority mode, the camera may be used with any lens that can be attached to the camera, as well as with the special series that has the additional linkages that permit shutter-priority operation.

If you have wide-ranging photographic interests including rapid action, close-ups, photomicrography, and perhaps a bit of astrophotography, for example, one dual-mode camera system could handle everything very conveniently and automatically. If you have fewer conflicting photographic requirements, you will probably find that either a shutter- or aperture-priority system will serve your purpose well and may cost a bit less.

Regardless of the type of automatic-exposure system built into a good SLR camera, most photographers feel more comfortable if some form of manual exposure control is also possible. This is because photographers, for aesthetic reasons, do not always wish to make a standardized "correct" exposure according to the built-in meter's built-in criteria, and because some lighting conditions and subjects cannot be rendered well by a built-in meter's simplistic approach to exposure control.

For this reason, automatic-exposure SLR cameras are nearly always equipped with an exposure override control that permits altering the amount of exposure by a predetermined increment or decrement. The range of adjustment normally runs from two stops underexposure to two stops overexposure. The override does not disconnect the camera's auto-exposure system, but simply biases it to provide more or less exposure than it would with the override in its normal "off" position. If you use an automatic-exposure camera with an override, check the override control before starting each new series of pictures, particularly if you are sharing the use of the camera. It is disheartening to discover that some of your best shots of the day were made while the override control was inadvertently set for unwanted over- or underexposure. To reduce the likelihood of the control being moved off neutral accidentally, many override controls are designed to lock in the "off" position, so that a separate release must be activated before the control can be budged. This is a desirable feature.

Although nearly all auto-exposure single-lens reflex cameras do provide a full range of manually set shutter speeds and lens apertures, some lose their metering ability when the auto-exposure system is disengaged. If a camera does lose metering on manual, you can set it to auto-exposure and use it as a light meter, noting the automatically selected *f*-stop or shutter speed from the finder display. Or, more conveniently, use a separate hand-held meter.

7

Cartridge-Loading 110 and 126 Cameras

Cameras that accept drop-in 110 or 126 film cartridges are the easiest to use if making snapshots conveniently is your primary photographic goal. And some of the more highly developed 110 models have found favor with serious hobbyists and professional photographers as "off-duty" cameras that are often small and light enough to drop in a pocket. Although cartridge-loading cameras range from elementary "box-camera" types that are factory set for use in bright outdoor light at moderate distances to zoom-lensed, electronically governed auto-exposure models, the key feature in all cases is ultra-simple film loading.

An astonishing number of camera users are either unable or unwilling to learn to load film into a camera correctly. The photofinishing industry has for years compiled gloomy data indicating that failure of the film to feed through the camera is a significant cause of spoiled pictures. Camera and film manufacturers have rightly concluded that the preferred solution to this problem, at least for the mass photographic market, is to minimize user participation in the loading process. The logical outgrowth is the film cartridge, which cannot be inserted into the camera incorrectly, and which spares the user the frustration of fumbling with an uncooperative, curling length of film. The cartridge automatically sets the camera's meter system, if the camera has a meter, for the proper film speed, and can be removed easily from the camera after the last shot has been made, without rewinding.

SIMPLE CARTRIDGE-LOADING CAMERAS

APERTURE AND SHUTTER SPEED

The least elaborate cartridge-loading cameras are the simplest to use because they have few controls to operate. They have fixed-aperture lenses, usually in the range of $f/5.6$ to $f/11$, and focus is factory set, normally providing a useful range of sharpness from about five feet to infinity. The shutter is generally a single- or two-speed type. Single-speed shutters operate at speeds ranging from 1/60 to 1/250 sec., depending on the lens aperture. Two-speed shutters generally provide a higher speed such as 1/125 or 1/250 sec. for outdoor shooting and a slower speed of about 1/45 or 1/50 sec. for indoor flash photography. The flash speed is often set automatically by attaching a Magicube or Flipflash to the camera. Although these elementary cameras do not incorporate built-in metering systems, they sometimes do use a light-sensing cell to trigger a warning signal that glows when the ambient light is too low to produce adequate exposure.

VIEWFINDERS

Simple optical viewfinders may have a bright frame to outline the picture area, or the extreme edges of the finder frame itself may serve that function. Finder information is normally limited to a "low-light/use-flash" signal.

FLASH

Flash photography may be done with Magicubes, Flipflash, or small separate or built-in electronic flash units, according to the design of the specific camera. Some cartridge cameras provide both a Magicube or Flipflash socket plus an attachment point for electronic flash, while others restrict the user to only one type of flash. In some models electronic flash units built into the camera body are convenient, but they add bulk to the camera as well as a few extra ounces. Unless you plan on making a fairly large number of flash pictures quite often, you may prefer a smaller, lighter camera without a built-in flash unit. As the lens aperture is fixed, acceptable flash exposures may be made within a fairly restricted distance range, which is specified in the owner's manual. The distance range is normally suited to indoor snapshot situations. If you expect to do much flash photography, check the owner's manual before you buy a camera to make sure that the camera's flash capabilities and usable distances are a reasonable match to your anticipated needs.

The simple cameras in this category can be surprisingly competent picture-takers when used with regard to their basic limitations. Because the shutter speeds tend to be moderate at best, these cameras are not well suited to photographing rapid action. Nor are they useful for available-light photography. But for extremely easy snapshot photography in good light, they are hard to beat. They also are good knockabout cameras for youngsters to take to camp or school events, because of their combination of easy operation and relatively low cost.

ADJUSTABLE CARTRIDGE-LOADING CAMERAS

BUILT-IN EXPOSURE SYSTEMS

Cartridge-loading cameras with built-in exposure-setting systems have proliferated to the point that just about any combination of features you might want—except for lens interchangeability—is represented by at least one model. Depending on the specific design, available shutter speeds may range from as long as ten seconds to as fast as 1/1000 sec., and lenses as fast as *f*/2 may be encountered. Auto-exposure systems may be programmed, with variable shutter and lens aperture, variable shutter with fixed lens aperture, or variable lens aperture and fixed shutter speed. Among the more elaborate cartridge cameras, auto-exposure systems are sometimes aperture-priority designs that let you choose an aperture, while the camera selects the appropriate shutter speed. Since aperture-priority auto-exposure allows you to induce the camera to set the highest possible shutter speed the conditions permit, cameras in this category have an edge over other types if you wish to freeze action without using flash.

FOCUSING SYSTEMS

Focusing systems include zone-focusing, coupled rangefinder, and one true single-lens reflex type, the Minolta 110 Zoom SLR. Zone-focusing cartridge cameras sometimes include a focusing indicator and zone symbols in the viewfinder for convenient reference at eye level. Focusing as close as three feet is generally possible, and some cameras provide built-in close-up

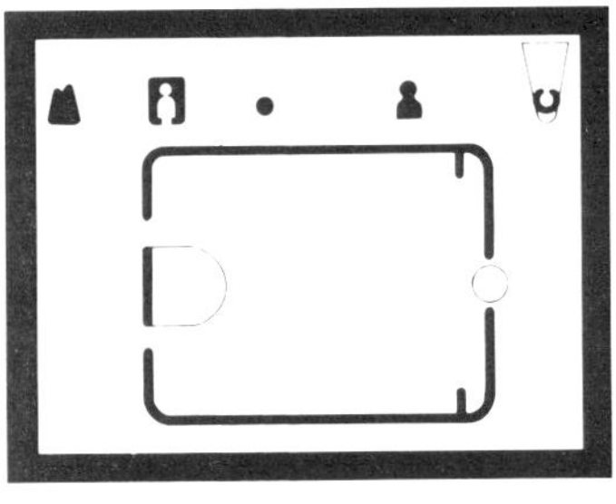

Zone-focus scale and indicator are visible above bright frame line of Minolta Pocket Autopak 470 110 cartridge camera. Other finder information includes low-light warning lamp in right frame line and warning flag (left) that pops into field when built-in close-up lens is positioned in optical path. Courtesy Minolta Corporation.

Minolta 110 Zoom SLR was first SLR camera designed for 110 film. Built-in zoom lens covers 25 mm to 50 mm range, normal to moderate telephoto for format. Slightly larger than other 110 cameras, it is also considerably more versatile. Courtesy Minolta Corporation.

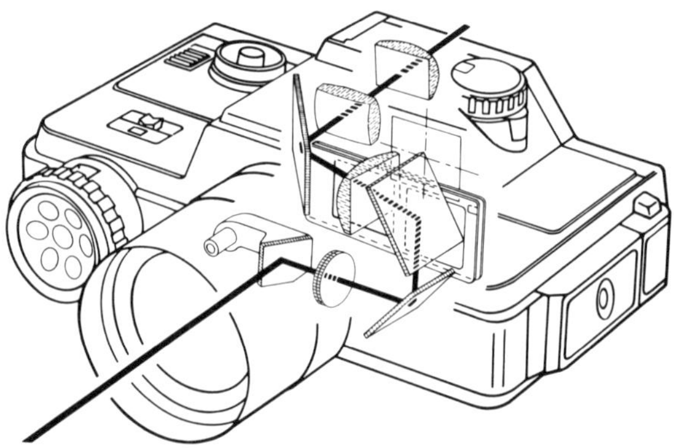

Diagram shows light path through lens and finder system of Minolta 110 Zoom SLR. Reflex mirror is at first bend in light path. It swings up through arc perpendicular to lens axis to clear path to film. Courtesy Minolta Corporation.

lenses for photography as close as about one-and-one-half feet. The Minolta 110 Zoom SLR focuses to approximately 11.3 inches with the aid of a built-in close-up element.

VIEWFINDERS

Most adjustable cartridge-loading cameras have optical viewfinders with a bright frame outlining the picture area. If the camera focuses close enough for parallax to be a consideration, the problem is most often handled simply with parallax correction marks appended to the bright frame line. A few finder systems compensate for parallax automatically by shifting the frame appropriately when the lens is set for close focus. This is more convenient than having to remember to use the correction marks at close-up distances, but is only significant if you actually expect to make a substantial number of tightly cropped pictures. The Minolta 110 Zoom SLR, as a true single-lens reflex camera, does not require a parallax correction system.

FLASH

The same range of flash options is offered for adjustable cartridge-loading cameras as for the less elaborate models. Flash exposure systems, however, may be considerably more versatile. Many adjust the camera's lens aperture for proper flash exposure to correspond to the distance from the camera to the subject. The camera's focusing mechanism is linked to the aperture-setting system when the camera is used in the flash mode. This system is basically simple and easy to use, and can produce excellent flash exposures provided the user does not exceed the maximum and minimum distances listed in the owner's manual. The workable distance ranges for these systems are more than adequate to deal with familiar interior flash situations.

AVAILABLE LIGHT POSSIBILITIES

If you prefer candid photography without flash, some adjustable cartridge-loading cameras are capable of producing acceptable available-light pictures because their metering systems are designed to function with ASA 400 films. The most useful combination for available-light shooting is a camera with a fairly large maximum lens aperture and a meter that can detect the ASA 400 meter-keying notch in cartridges containing high-speed film. A note of caution is in order here, though. The ASA 400 color films, while excellent materials, are perceptibly grainier

Unusually fast f/2 lens for 110 cartridge-loading camera distinguishes Canon 110ED-20. Camera also has coupled rangefinder focusing and a hot-shoe mount for cordless electronic flash. Courtesy Canon U.S.A., Inc.

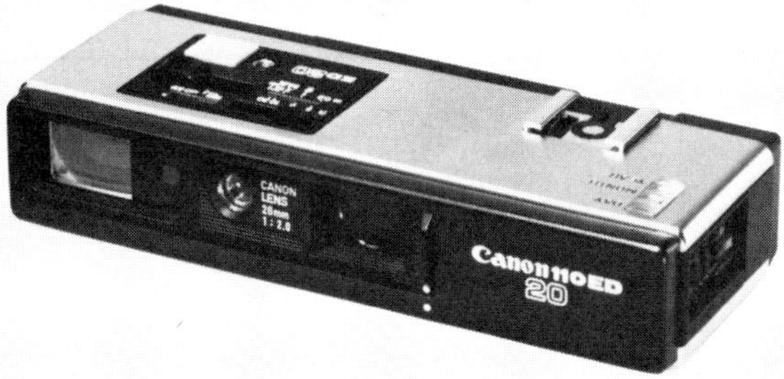

than the slower films normally spooled for cartridge-loading cameras. This does not cause a problem with small prints, but may become objectionable in 5″ × 7″ and 8″ × 10″ enlargements from 110 negatives.

Since the advent of ASA 400 film in 110 cartridges, all manufacturers would like to be able to claim that their cameras can use the high-speed film so as not to be left out. A few companies with cameras that lack the ability to adjust for ASA 400 film are stating simply that their cameras "accept" ASA 400 film, or wording to that effect. Technically, the claim is true, as the cartridge will fit. However, the film will be overexposed more than two full stops in most situations, as such cameras are unable to provide the different exposure settings required by the higher film speed. The manufacturers who do this assume that the film's latitude for overexposure will permit making a usable negative. The user gets a picture, although not as good quality as he might like, and the camera manufacturer avoids having to admit that the camera really isn't meant to be used with ASA 400 film. The moral is simply "buyer beware." If you expect to use ASA 400 film in 110 photography, make sure the camera you buy has a metering system and range of shutter speeds and lens openings that can actually use the greater film speed.

LENSES

As lens interchangeability is not yet a feature of 110 cartridge cameras, some models provide added optical versatility with built-in telephoto or zoom capability. Cameras with built-in

The switch on the Kodak Tele-Ektra 2 110 camera converts normal 22 mm lens to moderate telephoto 44 mm lens. Camera is shown with accessory electronic flash unit attached. Courtesy Eastman Kodak Company.

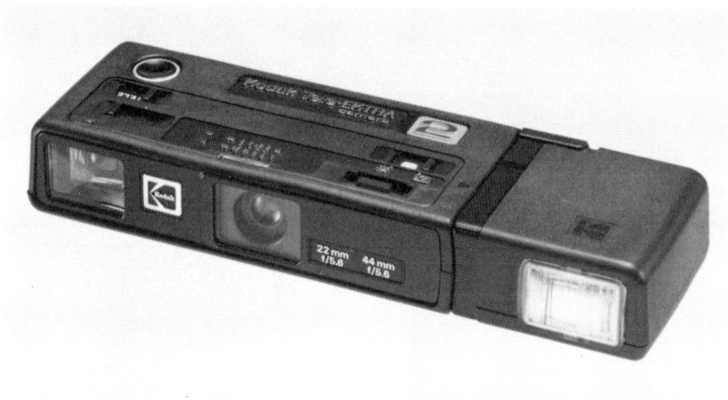

Telephoto capability via switch helps fill tiny 110 film frame with larger image for more effective snapshots. Courtesy Eastman Kodak Company.

telephoto systems (in addition to the normal lens) provide telephoto magnification of approximately 1.7× relative to the normal lens. This is roughly equivalent to an 85 mm short telephoto lens for a 35 mm full-frame camera, and is useful for making portraits and tightening up composition. Switching to the telephoto lens generally masks the viewfinder appropriately to indicate the telephoto lens field. The telephoto feature adds little additional bulk or weight to the camera.

Built-in zoom lenses provide a continuously variable field of view from normal to moderate telephoto, with magnifications of approximately 1.7× to 2×. They are quite useful for making precisely cropped pictures without too much back-and-forth movement needed to fill the frame as desired. Drawbacks, however, include relatively high cost, bulk that takes the camera out of the pocket category, and increased camera weight. Viewfinder systems include a built-in optical finder that zooms along with the lens, and a true SLR viewing system. The latter is preferable for close-up work, but both do well enough at moderate to far distances.

Desirable subsidiary features of cartridge-loading cameras include: warning signals in the viewfinder to tell you that the light is too low for a hand-held exposure, so use flash or a firm support; a signal to tell you that all bulbs have been expended in the Magicube or Flipflash mounted on the camera; and a battery-check circuit to show that the camera batteries are in good condition. If you're interested in trying low-light photography, look for both a tripod-mounting socket and a cable release socket. In cameras that have built-in lens covers, an interlock that prevents tripping the shutter while the lens is covered is desirable.

The preceding discussion of cartridge-loading cameras has been based largely on current 110 models. Much of it is applicable to larger 126 cartridge cameras, which are at best obsolescent and fading fast, although often capable of producing good results. If you are about to buy a cartridge-loading camera, it's probably advisable to stick to the better 110 types. If you are currently using a 126 camera and are happy with the results you get, you may as well stay with it, as few 110 models are likely to offer more, other than the ability to fit into a pocket.

8

35 mm and Roll-Film Cameras with Noninterchangeable Lenses

Easy-to-use 35 mm and roll-film cameras with non-interchangeable lenses and optical viewfinders are the "sensible shoes" of snapshot photography. This type of camera was once associated primarily with medium-format roll film, but the pendulum has swung to favor 35 mm almost to the exclusion of larger versions. Early 35 mm models were about the same size as more elaborate 35 mm interchangeable-lens cameras, but current designs tend to be quite compact and seriously rival some of the medium-size or larger 110 cartridge cameras with respect to convenient carrying and even pocketability.

THE SIMPLEST

FOCUSING

Basic cameras are most often equipped with a non-interchangeable lens of normal or slightly wide-angle focal length, with a maximum aperture of approximately *f*/2.8. Both faster and slower lenses are occasionally encountered, but *f*/2.8 seems to be the standard number for this category. Focusing is a matter of estimating distance to the subject and then setting the lens with reference to a scale of distance or zone symbols representing distances. The distances and/or symbols frequently appear on the lens barrel. Some cameras also present focus-

Compact 35 mm Minolta Hi-matic G has programmed automatic exposure range from 1/30 sec. at f/2.8 to 1/650 sec. at f/14. Semi-wide-angle 38 mm lens has enough depth of field to make zone focusing feasible. Courtesy Minolta Corporation.

setting distances or symbols in the viewfinder, with a moving indicator to show the distance to which the lens is set. This is a worthwhile feature, as it facilitates setting focus with the camera at eye level and also serves as a reminder to focus. Focusing distances range from infinity to about three feet. Closer focusing is not really practical without a rangefinder or other focusing aid, as a minor error in estimating distance can cause a major loss of sharpness in close-ups. At the moderate distances that typify most snapshot photography, estimation is a practical way to obtain adequately sharp images.

SHUTTERS

Shutters are generally between-the-lens or behind-the-lens leaf types, with top speeds of approximately 1/500 sec. Slow-speed capability may end at 1/30 sec. or may run to several seconds, depending on the elaborateness of the exposure system and the shutter design. Electronic shutter timing is quite common now, although the simplest cameras in this category still use traditional mechanically timed shutters.

EXPOSURE CONTROL

Exposure control is normally automatic and programmed, with a light-sensing cell built into the camera body or situated in the front of the lens mount. Meter settings generally provide for film speeds from ASA 25 to ASA 400 or 500, which is adequate for most applications. Designers assume correctly that users of these cameras are unlikely to need extra-high ASA settings.

FLASH

For photography with electronic flash units, synchronization is often achieved through a hot-shoe mounting fixture built onto the camera, which both holds the flash unit in place and automatically makes electrical contact with it. Only flash units with mounts wired for cordless contact are suitable for hot-shoe operation. Although most small electronic flash units now feature hot-shoe synchronization, double-check before buying a flash unit to assure that it and the camera are compatible. Some cameras also have separate flash contacts for PC-tipped synchronizing cords, which allow use with nearly every cord-synched flash unit ever produced. Few simple 35 mm cameras provide separate synchronization for expendable-bulb flash, but many do permit use, via the electronic-flash X-synch circuit, of small flashbulbs such as the all-glass peanut types and flash-cubes in suitable adapters.

The simplest, and least versatile, flash exposure systems merely indicate by owner's manual or a camera scale what range of distances will produce usable exposures with flash sources of various output. More elaborate flash systems will adjust the lens aperture appropriately with changes in the camera's focus setting, providing a considerably expanded useful distance range for flash photography. If your use of flash will be only occasional, the former system, or non-system, may be adequate. If you expect flash pictures to play an important part in your use of the camera, seek a model that allows manual flash settings or one that has a reasonably versatile automatic system.

VIEWFINDERS

The viewfinder usually contains a bright frame outlining the picture area, possibly with a focusing scale and indicator at one edge. Parallax correction marks are included when the camera's close-focusing capability makes parallax correction desirable. Depending on the sophistication of the exposure system, actual exposure settings that are being automatically set may be indicated, or you may be informed by warning lamps or moving indicator that there is too much or too little light for proper exposure. A signal may also warn that an automatic exposure will be too slow to hand-hold. A battery-check lamp may be visible in the finder or elsewhere on the camera, if the camera has a test circuit. As a rule, the more complex the camera, and the higher the price, the more information you will get in the finder. Cameras with automatic flash exposure systems may have a finder signal that indicates the camera is operating in the flash mode.

Compact 35 mm cameras are handy for candid grab-shooting. Automatic exposure allows fast, effortless operation, and full-frame 35 mm format enlarges well in color or black-and-white.

DELUXE MODELS

APERTURE AND SHUTTER SPEEDS

Deluxe-model compact cameras are generally similar to the basic versions, but offer greater versatility and, sometimes, more opportunity for user control of what's happening inside. Lenses are about the same focal length, but are often faster, with maximum apertures in the area of *f*/1.7 to *f*/2. Shutter-speed ranges are expanded, too, with speeds as slow as ten seconds and as fast as 1/1000 sec. often available. The faster lens apertures and expanded range of shutter speeds give these more elaborate models a decided edge in producing usable exposures in marginal lighting conditions that would be beyond the capabilities of the more basic cameras. Auto-exposure programming generally makes good use of the wider choice of shutter speeds and *f*-stops, with more emphasis on using higher shutter speeds as lighting conditions and film speed permit. This makes these cameras better choices when your subject matter will favor action or low-light situations without flash.

RANGEFINDERS

Another plus for the deluxe compacts is that they nearly all have coupled rangefinders. Focusing with the coincident-type rangefinders used is simple and effortless, and far more accurate than estimating distance. This advantage shows up clearly in pictures made at close distances and/or in dim light, when there is little depth of field to cover focusing errors. And rangefinder focusing also results in generally better and more consistent flash exposures with cameras that provide flash-exposure automation by coupling the lens aperture to the focus setting when using flash.

Except for the desirable addition of the central rangefinder focusing area, viewfinders in deluxe compacts are similar to those of the basic cameras. A few deluxe models provide automatic parallax correction by shifting the bright frame appropriately as the lens is focused on closer subjects. If you expect to do much close-range photography, this is a convenience, but in most cases using the parallax-correction marks will do as well.

ADDITIONAL FEATURES

Some cameras in this class have a feature described as a "safe-load signal," which is intended to reassure you that film is feeding properly through the camera. It generally consists of a small glassed-in window on the camera body that provides a peep at an indicator that bobs or creeps a short distance as the film advances. It's a nice touch, but really unnecessary. You can check on film feed easily enough by watching the knob of the rewind shaft while advancing film. If the rewind rotates, film is stripping out of the film chamber and feeding through the camera properly.

An odd feature that a few manufacturers resurrect every now and then is a built-in picture-dating device. This usually consists of user-set number wheels that can be adjusted to expose the date or a numerical code onto a corner of the film frame when the exposure is made. These gadgets usually have an "off" setting that permits making pictures without number imprints, presumably on occasions that you'd rather not pinpoint too precisely.

Many of the cameras in the upper echelon of this category are equipped with self-timers. They are simply delayed-action tripping mechanisms that let you activate the self-timer 6 to 12 seconds before the self-timer triggers the exposure. The absence of a self-timer should not count against an otherwise desirable camera. Almost any camera with a conventional cable-release socket can be fitted with a removable accessory self-timer.

A feature worth looking for, if the camera will be used by someone who would like to experiment with photographic technique, is a switch permitting manual exposure setting. The auto-exposure system does the routine drudge work, and the manual mode lets you set shutter speeds and *f*-stops independently when you want a special effect.

Overall, the features associated with 35 mm and roll-film non-interchangeable-lens cameras provide about the same level of picture-taking capability as the better 110 cartridge-loading cameras, but with one major difference. The larger frame sizes of the larger formats are capable of yielding significantly superior picture quality when enlargements of 5″ × 7″ and beyond will be made. This is especially true when films will be subjected to mass-production "drugstore" photofinishing, rather than custom or careful home processing. Another advantage of stepping up from the cartridge formats is the greater variety of films available in 35 mm and roll sizes, thus offering more options for matching film characteristics to photographic situations as well as to personal taste.

From the standpoint of optical versatility, most non-interchangeable-lens 35 mm and roll-film cameras have no advantage over the cartridge cameras. In fact, some of the cartridge-loaders offering close-up, telephoto, or zoom-lens capability have an edge in this area.

Still another factor to consider if you're undecided about whether to buy a good 110 cartridge or 35 mm compact camera is the matter of which you find more comfortable to use. You may find that the "conventional" shape of the 35 mm camera feels better to you than the harmonica styling of most 110 cameras, or vice versa.

9

35 mm and Roll-Film Rangefinder Cameras with Interchangeable Lenses

35 MM FORMAT

As a class, 35 mm rangefinder cameras with interchangeable lenses were for several decades the undisputed first choice of photographers who needed fast-handling, versatile, handholdable equipment. Although largely eclipsed by the increasingly popular SLR design, and in 35 mm verging on extinction, with only one remaining brand in production, the interchangeable-lens rangefinder camera remains a desirable and viable means of making pictures. In roll-film formats, it is still playing an active role in professional photography, and is much favored by wedding photographers.

The classic 35 mm rangefinder camera of recent vintage consists of a fairly small but rugged body housing a focal-plane shutter, viewfinder/rangefinder system, and a film transport/rewind mechanism. The front of the body is fitted with a bayonet or screw-threaded lens mount. Except for several Leica models that offer through-the-lens metering, built-in meters are uncommon.

SHUTTER

Shutter-speed ranges are commonly one second through 1/1000 sec., plus "Bulb" for long exposures. Electronic-flash synchronization speed is usually 1/50 or 1/60 sec., and focal-

Interchangeable-lens rangefinder cameras such as Leica M4-2 are extremely easy to focus, fast handling, and superbly responsive. They are very quiet, and well suited to candid shooting at close range. Lens shown is extraordinarily fast 50 mm Noctilux, with maximum aperture of f/1. Smaller f/1.4 and f/2 lenses are more usual. Courtesy E. Leitz, Inc.

plane flashbulbs are often usable at all speeds, but check the owner's manual or the distributor's service department to be sure. Most rangefinder cameras made by Leitz, Nikon, and Canon have very quiet shutters. This hushed quality is still prized by photographers who work candidly or in environments where obtrusive camera-clicking would be unwelcome, such as movie sets or concert halls. The beautifully made pre-World War II and the post-war Contax rangefinders are an exception to the rule of super-quiet shutters; their guillotine-style, vertical-travel metal shutters make a distinctive and distinctly audible sound.

VIEWFINDER/RANGEFINDER

The combined optical viewfinder/rangefinder system in top-of-the-line models consists of a bright frame for the 50 mm (sometimes 35 mm or 40 mm) lens, which moves appropriately as the lens is focused to provide automatic parallax correction. Additional bright frames outlining fields of view of various interchangeable lenses within the manufacturer's line pop into the viewfinder when selected manually by switch or when the appropriate lens is mounted onto the camera. Frame lines for accessory lenses are also usually parallax-corrected. To avoid cluttering the finder system, frame lines are normally incorporated for what the designers considered to be the most popular focal lengths. A typical combination would be 35 mm, 50 mm, and 85 mm or 90 mm frames, or 50 mm, 85 mm or 90 mm, and 135 mm bright frames. Depending on the specific camera model, wide-angle lenses starting with 35 mm or 28 mm usually require the use of a separate optical finder mounted in an accessory shoe on the top deck of the camera.

The rangefinder built into the finder couples to all lenses intended for the camera, usually permitting focusing as close as two-and-one-half to three feet with normal and moderate wide-angle lenses. When using lenses for which no built-in finder frame is provided, the subject must be framed first through the accessory viewfinder, and the lens focused afterward by shifting the eye to the main viewfinder, in which the rangefinder spot is visible. This procedure is much easier and faster to follow than to describe, and one can pick up the habit quickly. Accessory

Viewfinder of 35 mm interchangeable-lens rangefinder camera may have built-in field frames for lens focal lengths of 35 mm, 50 mm, and 90 mm, for example. Not all frames would normally be in sight simultaneously.

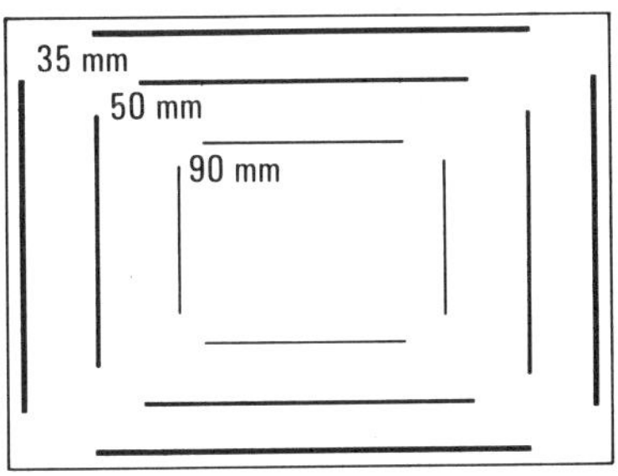

External frame-selector switch of some Leicas brings various field frames into view to help determine which lens focal length will frame subject best. This is more convenient than having to change lenses just to preview subject.

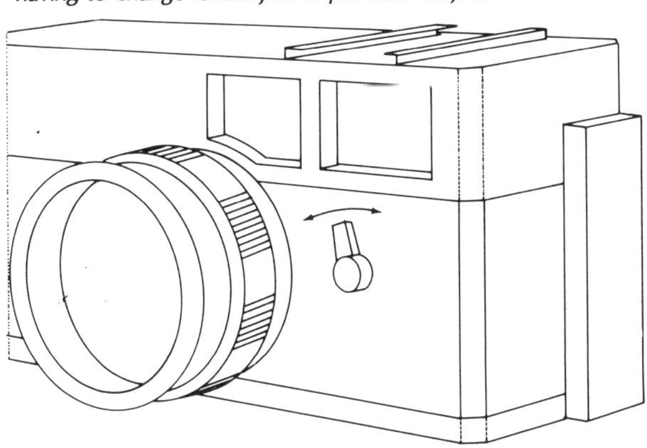

viewfinders may or may not incorporate a means of correcting for parallax, depending on the focal lengths and minimum focusing distances of the lenses they are meant to accompany.

LENSES

Most interchangeable-lens 35 mm rangefinder cameras accept rangefinder-coupled accessory lenses from 19 mm or 21 mm extreme wide-angles to 135 mm moderate telephotos. Most users seem to concur that the viewfinder/rangefinder systems are not at their best with 135 mm lenses, as the framed area in the finder within which one composes the picture tends to be somewhat small. The 85 mm or 90 mm frames, however, outline a large enough portion of the finder image to allow convenient composition. The consensus is that 35 mm rangefinder cameras are lovely to use with short telephotos but are difficult with 135's. With normal lenses, viewing and focusing are extremely convenient, and the same applies to viewing and focusing with any wide-angles that do not require the use of an accessory finder.

In days gone by when extreme wide-angle lenses were almost invariably rather slow, rangefinder cameras were the preferred types for wide-angle work. Their viewing brightness and focusing ease put them far ahead of other systems with the

Leitz Visoflex III reflex housing with pentaprism finder converts Leica M-series cameras to SLR viewing and focusing for long-lens and close-up photography. Only 135 mm and shorter lenses are normally available with rangefinder-coupled focusing mounts for 35 mm rangefinder cameras. Courtesy E. Leitz, Inc.

Reflex housing between 200 mm lens and camera body turned lightweight 35 mm rangefinder camera into heavyweight SLR for this telephoto shot. Although combination works very well, a true SLR camera is more convenient for long-lens work.

dim wide-angles of the time. Today's high-speed extreme wide-angles have evened out the difference somewhat, but it is still not uncommon to see a photojournalist work with a rangefinder camera for wide-angle shots and one or more SLR cameras for telephoto shots. It's a natural division of labor. A wide-angle lens is difficult to focus accurately and decisively on a ground-glass screen because its greater depth of field at any given distance tends to make everything look fairly sharp. The rangefinder focuses mechanically and is unaffected by the lens' depth of field. A telephoto lens is usually easy to focus on a ground-glass screen because its relatively shallower depth of field at any given distance makes in-focus and out-of-focus areas readily identifiable. As noted earlier, rangefinders are less convenient to use

Documentary photography and photojournalism are natural applications for interchangeable-lens rangefinder cameras.

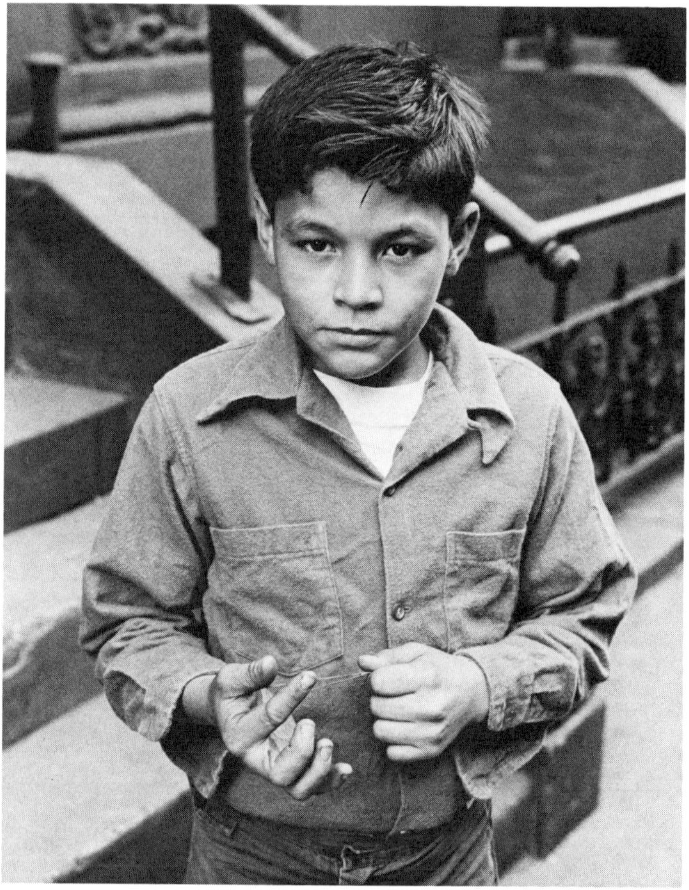

with longer lenses, and are simply incapable of providing the necessary degree of focusing accuracy with focal lengths longer than 135 mm with 35 mm cameras, or longer than about 250 mm with medium-format roll-film models.

On balance, the 35 mm interchangeable-lens rangefinder camera is close to being the ideal working tool for the photographer who wants a relatively lightweight, compact, quiet, rugged camera that focuses fast and accurately in almost any light level with lenses from extreme wide-angle to short or moderate telephoto. It is well suited to the needs of the photojournalist or documentary photographer, for example, who must work quickly, decisively, and unobtrusively. In terms of limitations, 35 mm and larger-format rangefinder cameras are restricted in the range of lenses they will accept and are clumsy to use for close-ups or telephotography. Although accessories are available to adapt some rangefinder cameras to through-the-lens viewing and focusing, utility and convenience are less than a true single-lens reflex or view camera might offer in a specific application.

MEDIUM FORMAT

Medium-format rangefinder cameras offer the viewing and focusing advantages described in conjunction with 35 mm cameras, plus the larger picture sizes associated with 120/220 roll film. Shutters are normally between-the-lens leaf-type designs,

Interchangeable-lens rangefinder cameras for 120/220 roll film, such as Rapid Omega 200, combine advantages of bright viewing and fast focusing with substantially greater negative sizes that require less enlargement. Courtesy Rapid Omega Division, Berkey Marketing Companies.

so each interchangeable lens has its own built-in shutter. As with most leaf shutters, top speeds are in the range of 1/400 to 1/500 sec., and electronic flash synchronization is possible at all speeds. Flexible flash synchronization makes it fairly easy to combine flash and ambient-light exposures when fill flash is needed to lighten shadow areas in outdoor photography. And high synchronization speeds help reduce or eliminate the ghost-image effects of ambient light when flash is desired as the sole source of photographic illumination. Additionally, the photographer can see through the optical viewfinder whether or not the flash unit has fired. With single-lens reflex cameras, the raised mirror blacks out the view through the finder during the moment of exposure, so the photographer may not be able to tell if the flash unit has triggered properly.

Drawbacks of the medium-format rangefinder cameras are the relatively limited choice of lenses available for any given model, lack of high-speed lenses, unsuitability for close-ups and telephotography, and comparative bulk and weight of both camera bodies and accessory lenses. These negative aspects might be significant to the photographer looking for a general-purpose, do-everything camera system. But the drawbacks are largely irrelevant to the many professionals who need rugged, portable, hand-held cameras suitable for capturing the action at weddings, confirmations, bar mitzvahs, dinner dances, and award ceremonies, to mention just a few of the events where you're likely to find a medium-format rangefinder camera earning its keep.

10

35 mm and Roll-Film Single-Lens Reflex Cameras

Single-lens reflex cameras for 35 mm and roll film are, collectively, the current darlings of amateur and professional photographers. Although you can dredge up all manner of esoteric theories to explain the popularity of SLR cameras, the key reasons are probably versatility and the ground-glass image.

From the standpoint of versatility, top-quality SLR's are true *system* cameras, in which the basic camera body can be accessorized to the limits of the photographer's needs, imagination, or bank account. The widest, longest, fastest, and most innovative lenses are available for SLR's. The most convenient manual and/or automatic through-the-lens metering systems are found in SLR's. The most elaborate special-purpose finder systems are available for SLR's. A wide range of accessory automatic winders and motor drives are available for SLR's. An incredible array of close-up accessories is available for SLR's. Consequently, there are few photographic tasks that cannot be tackled successfully with a single-lens reflex camera and suitable accessories.

The significance of viewing and focusing on a ground-glass screen that shows the image formed by the lens that will take the picture cannot be overestimated. Although the SLR's ground-glass screen provides a dimmer image that is often harder to focus than the bright image seen through an optical viewfinder, the SLR image relates directly and strongly to the image that will be recorded on film. With the lens stopped down to the aperture

Viewing and focusing on a ground glass through the lens that will actually take the picture aid precise composition and alignment of picture elements relative to each other and to the camera.

that will be used to make the picture, depth of field may be appraised visually, and adjusted to best advantage. Viewing is free of parallax with any lens focal length and at any distance from the subject. In short, the photographer may see in the SLR viewfinder a surprisingly good preview of the finished photograph, not only in terms of vertical and horizontal placement of objects within the frame, but also with respect to depth of field. The SLR viewfinder does an excellent job of immediately showing the photographer how a three-dimensional scene will be rendered on a two-dimensional surface. And that is basically what photography is all about.

Freedom from parallax and ground-glass viewing and focusing in a convenient "package" make 35 mm SLR's top choice for shooting with long tele lenses. Here a 200 mm lens allowed filling frame with a big image without approaching intrusively.

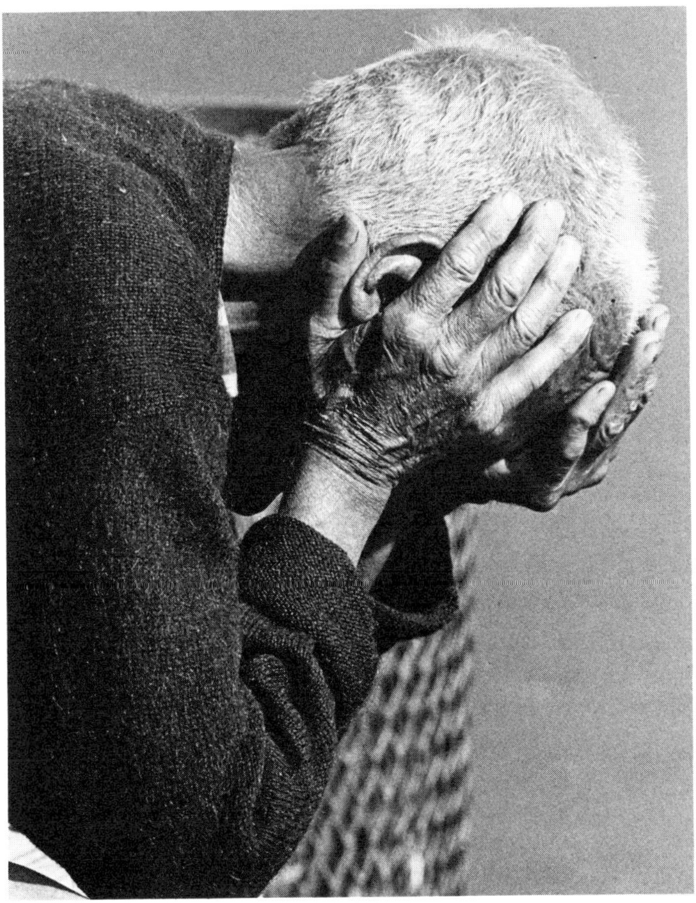

35 MM SLR'S

All current major-brand 35 mm SLR's are designed primarily for eye-level operation, feature lens interchangeability via bayonet or screw-thread mounts (one manufacturer uses a so-called breech-lock mount that combines desirable features of both systems), and have instant-return reflex mirrors and automatic lens diaphragm operation with most accessory lenses. The instant-return mirror flips up out of the path of image-forming light a moment before the shutter opens and returns automatically to the viewing/focusing position in the optical path as soon as the shutter closes. An automatic lens diaphragm remains fully open for maximum ground-glass brightness during viewing and focusing regardless of the *f*-stop that has been preselected with the aperture-setting ring. When the shutter release is pressed, the diaphragm stops down to the preselected aperture before the shutter opens. It reopens for bright viewing and focusing as soon as the shutter closes. Earlier SLR models often had semi-automatic mirror operation. Operating the shutter release raised the mirror automatically, but it would remain up, preventing viewing and focusing, until the film was advanced to the next frame. Nonautomatic lens diaphragms were also the rule with early SLR's. Both fully manual and preset-diaphragm lenses

In diagram of 35 mm SLR operating cycle, (A) is lens diaphragm, (B) is reflex mirror, and (C) is film frame. Focal-plane shutter ahead of film is not shown. Before exposure, lens diaphragm is fully open for bright viewing and focusing. Mirror reflects viewing/focusing image through finder system. Shutter is closed. During exposure, lens diaphragm stops down automatically to preset aperture. Reflex mirror flips out of light path and also prevents light entering through finder eyepiece from reaching film chamber. Shutter opens to expose film, then closes. Mirror returns automatically to viewing position, and lens diaphragm reopens automatically to maximum aperture.

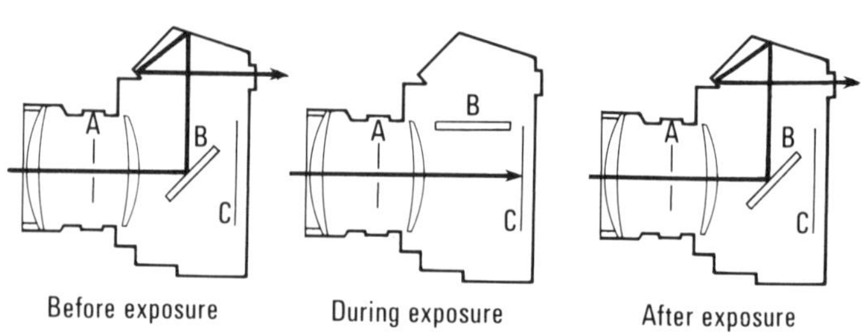

Extreme versatility through interchangeable lenses and accessories is strong suit of 35 mm SLR cameras. Array of Nikon system equipment includes Nikon and Nikkormat cameras, lenses, finders, focusing screens, motor drives, close-up accessories, and intervalometers. Most major 35 mm SLR systems provide more or less similar options. Courtesy Nikon Inc. (EPOI).

require that the photographer remember to close the diaphragm to the appropriate aperture before exposure, then reopen it to brighten the finder image prior to viewing and focusing the next picture.

SHUTTERS

Nearly all current 35 mm SLR's have mechanically or electronically timed focal-plane shutters with top speeds of 1/1000 or 1/2000 sec. A few budget-priced models may have a 1/500-sec. top speed. Unless you plan to photograph sports or other subjects involving rapid motion, a top speed of 1/500 sec. is amply fast. In fact, most photographers find that with medium-speed film outdoors, they seldom have an opportunity to shoot faster than 1/250 sec. Shutter-timed slow speeds generally run down to one second with mechanically timed shutters and as long as 30 seconds with some electronically timed shutters. Shutter-timed long-exposure capability can be convenient, but the fact remains that timing exposures of five seconds or longer duration is easily done with any timepiece that has a sweep second hand.

A few older 35 mm SLR's have behind-the-lens leaf shutters, with speeds generally ranging from a top of 1/500 sec. to one second at the slow end. These cameras, although often good general-purpose picture-takers, have always suffered from the rather limited lens interchangeability imposed by the shutter mechanism and its location. They are also limited in their ability to accept close-up accessories.

EXPOSURE CONTROL

Exposure-control systems range from none at all (you set shutter speed and *f*-stop according to a separate exposure meter or your intuition) to the most innovative through-the-lens systems offering total automation plus exposure override plus optional manual control.

From a practical point of view, it doesn't make much difference whether the metering system uses CdS, Si, or GAP cells, unless the camera is an auto-exposure model that will be used with an automatic winder or electric motor drive. The noticeably faster response time of Si and GAP meters lets them keep up with rapidly changing light levels and subject brightnesses that may be encountered, for example, when shooting a continuous-run sequence of a racing car whizzing from a brightly lighted section of track to a shadowed area. With manually set exposure systems and nonmotorized automatic systems, there is less need for ultra-fast meter response, and CdS is likely to prove more than adequate.

VIEWFINDERS

The viewfinders of 35 mm SLR's range from the austere to opulent in terms of displayed data and the manner of presentation. Economy models with manually set exposure systems usually show little other than the meter needle and a moving indicator or fixed reference to which it must be matched. More elaborate models may show the shutter speed and/or lens speed to which the camera is set. Auto-exposure cameras normally indicate at least the camera-selected exposure variable. That is, an aperture-priority camera will show the automatically set shutter speed, and a shutter-priority camera will show the automatically selected lens aperture. In addition, top-of-the-line models may show the manually set shutter speed or *f*- stop. Other types of finder displays may light up to tell you the scene is too bright or too dim for the preset shutter speed or lens aperture, or for the meter to operate accurately. Some recent electronic SLR's also have flash ready-lamps in the finder that light up or blink when a specially compatible electronic flash of the same brand is ready to fire while attached to the camera.

PREVIEWING DEPTH OF FIELD

Nearly all 35 mm SLR's have a depth-of-field preview button or lever that stops the lens down to the preset aperture when it is activated, and allows the lens to open up again when

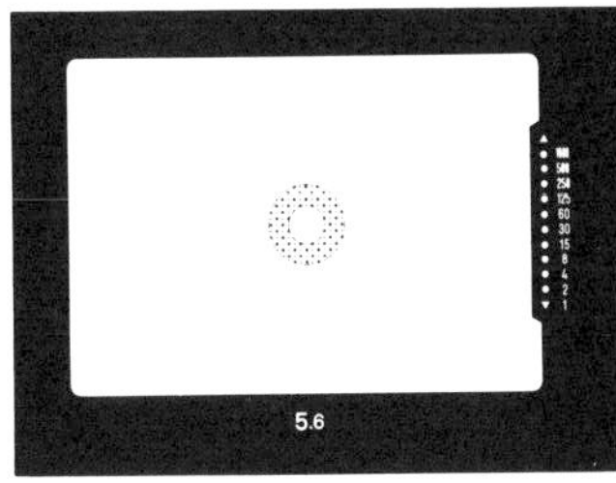

Minolta's 35 mm auto-exposure XD-11 is first SLR to offer choice of aperture-priority, shutter-priority, or manual exposure setting. In aperture-priority mode, finder readout shows aperture to which photographer has set lens (bottom). LED's light alongside shutter-speed scale (right) to indicate speed camera is setting automatically. Courtesy Minolta Corporation.

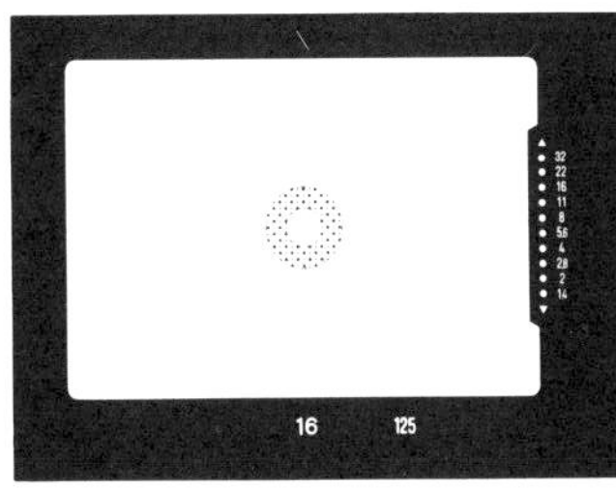

When XD-11 is set for shutter-priority automatic exposures, finder readouts show aperture to which photographer has set lens (normally minimum aperture), and shutter speed photographer has selected. LED's at right light up to indicate actual lens aperture camera is setting automatically. Courtesy Minolta Corporation.

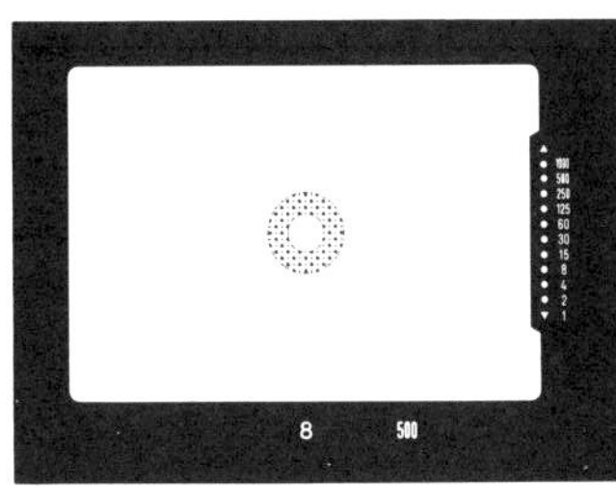

With XD-11 switched to manual mode, finder readouts show manually set lens aperture and shutter speed. LED's light up alongside shutter-speed scale to indicate speed recommended by camera's metering system. Courtesy Minolta Corporation.

released. This makes it easier to view the effects of depth of field at various aperture settings. A few 35 mm SLR's have no provision for previewing depth of field. Previewing depth of field is not necessary with most subjects most of the time. The ability to do so, however, is vital in close-up photography, where depth of field is minimal at best, and in long-lens photography, where controlling depth of field can make or break a picture. If close-up and/or telephoto photography are important to you, steer clear of any SLR that won't let you preview depth of field. For less specialized photography, previewing will probably not be missed, and some of the SLR's lacking this feature are in other respects pleasant and capable machines to use.

Several SLR's accept interchangeable finders. Minolta 35 mm SLR is shown with pentaprism incorporating through-the-lens auto-exposure metering system. In front (from left) are: plain pentaprism finder; folding waist-level finder; and rigid high-magnification finder. Courtesy Minolta Corporation.

Several 35 mm SLR's have interchangeable viewfinders. Normally, an eye-level pentaprism finder, with or without a built-in metering system, is considered the standard finder. The eye-level pentaprism is certainly the most popular for general use, as it presents an upright, unreversed view of the subject. For special applications, however, other finders may be easier to use. Making the camera finder removable also makes it possible to change ground-glass focusing screens easily, and cameras with interchangeable viewfinders also feature interchangeable focusing screens. Changing focusing screens lets you choose a type of screen that you prefer. It also lets you change screens as necessary for most efficient viewing and focusing with different types of lenses and in various photographic situations. Some 35 mm SLR's with fixed, nonremovable pentaprisms allow changing focusing screens through the lens mount opening of the camera body. The obvious advantages of finder and focusing screen interchangeability are that you can virtually custom-tailor the camera's viewing and focusing system to your preferences and working needs.

OTHER FEATURES

Some 35 mm SLR's have a control called a *mirror lock,* which allows raising the reflex mirror manually before making the exposure. The object is to reduce to a minimum any vibration that might impair image sharpness during tripod-mounted photography, particularly when using long lenses or making close-ups. If you expect to specialize in either area, a mirror lock is an extremely desirable feature. Incidentally, in recent years, several manufacturers have quietly eliminated the mirror lock from various of their SLR models to try to hold down costs.

Except for stripped-down economy models, most current 35 mm SLR's have *self-timers*. In a few cameras, the self-timer can serve as a functional substitute for a mirror lock when photographing static subjects. This is because some self-timer mechanisms trigger mirror movement several seconds before releasing the shutter, allowing mirror-related vibrations to dissipate prior to exposure. Manufacturers' literature seldom specifies whether the self-timer trips the mirror at the beginning or end of the self-timer cycle, but you can determine this easily for yourself when handling the camera. It's a minor advantage, but an advantage nonetheless.

Multiple exposures were once the bane of photographers, so camera designers developed reliable interlocks between the shutter-cocking and film-transport systems. Ironically, now that all 35 mm SLR's have simultaneous shutter cocking and film

SLR viewing lets photographer see world as lens on camera sees it, and is conducive to making "designy" pictures. Here, a 135 mm lens compressed rows of chairs into a strange pattern. Potential for pattern would have been less apparent to photographer had he been looking through finder of a rangefinder camera.

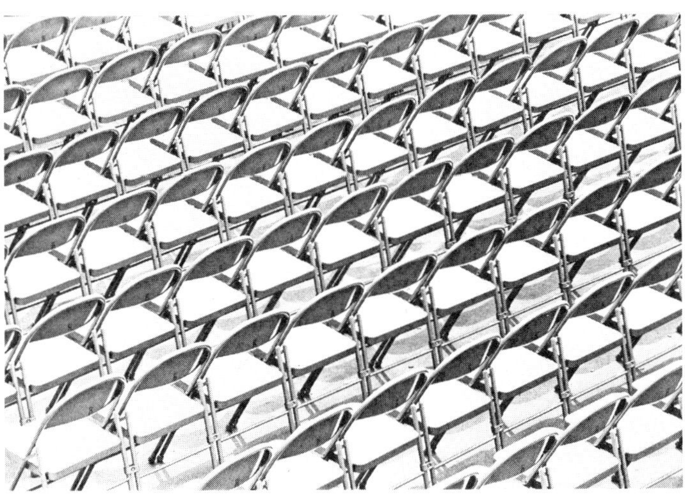

advance, eliminating inadvertent multiple exposures, the deliberate multiple exposure is coming into vogue. Consequently, more and more 35 mm SLR's have a special multiple-exposure control that allows recocking the shutter easily without moving the film in the camera. The most desirable multiple-exposure systems must be reactivated for each additional exposure on a frame, preventing you from accidentally making 36 exposures on one piece of film. It's also an advantage if the multiple-exposure control deactivates the film counter, preventing it from misrepresenting additional exposures on a single film frame as additional frames exposed.

A feature to consider well in advance of the time you may decide to use it is the camera's ability to accept an accessory *motorized film winder* or heavy-duty *motor drive.* Many SLR manufacturers market camera models that are quite similar in overall features and performance except that some are designed to accept an add-on motorized film advance. If you are certain that you will never want the rapid-fire sequence capability or just plain luxury provided by an electric surrogate thumb, you can often save a little money by buying the model that cannot be motorized. Conversely, if the nature of your photography is such that you'll eventually want an electric motor drive or power winder, it's economically advisable to pay a few dollars more at the outset for motor compatibility. It will cost less than having to buy an additional camera body later on.

A feature of some automatic-exposure SLR's is a switch that moves internal, *lighttight blinds* in front of the eyepiece, blacking out the finder. During tripod-mounted photography, covering the eyepiece prevents stray light from entering the finder and causing erroneous metering and exposure. During hand-held photography, the photographer's eye is normally close enough to the finder eyepiece to shade it adequately. When using a tripod, though, the photographer is not necessarily in a position to block the eyepiece effectively, so some sort of eyepiece blind is used. Switch-operated internal blinds are the most convenient. Lower-priced auto-exposure SLR's are often supplied with black plastic caps that slip onto the frame around the eyepiece. Capping the eyepiece is effective, but less convenient than flicking a switch. Unless you expect to work with a tripod often, the increment of convenience is academic.

The above enumeration of camera features by no means exhausts the possibilities, but does represent some of the more functional facets of current 35 mm SLR's. In addition, these cameras are differentiated in terms of size, weight, and a host of handling characteristics that fall conveniently in the grab-bag category of human engineering. Like human beings, 35 mm SLR's, despite basic similarities, do come in a wide range of variations. Analyzing your current needs and future intentions will help you select combinations of features that are useful. However, the combinations are likely to occur in several or even many SLR models. Your ultimate decision should be based not only on price and reputation, but also on how the camera feels to you. No matter what is "right" with an SLR, if you don't feel comfortable with it, it's wrong for you.

ROLL-FILM SLR'S

Roll-film SLR cameras occupy an anomalous position. The photographers who use them often do so out of necessity. With 120 and 220 film formats ranging from 4.5 × 6 cm to 6 × 7 cm, they provide roughly three to five times the film area of a 35 mm frame, yet the camera remains small enough and light enough for hand-held photography. However, the typical medium-format SLR is still no lightweight compared to its 35 mm counterpart, nor does it offer the almost unlimited opportunities for accessories—and versatility—associated with the smaller format. On the other hand, it does provide considerably more portability, convenience, and faster operation than large-format cameras that use sheet film. Thus the medium-format SLR is a compromise.

Relative sizes of 35 mm, 6 × 6 cm, and 6 × 7 cm frames show that roll-film formats provide enough additional image area to justify greater size and weight of cameras and accessories for certain applications.

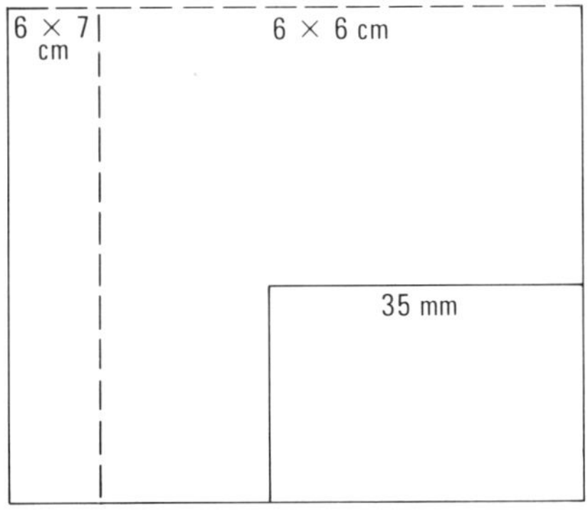

With standard waist-level finder, TLR's viewing/focusing image is upright but laterally reversed. This can be a nuisance when trying to follow moving subjects. An interchangeable prism finder cures problem.

VIEWFINDERS

Nearly all roll-film SLR cameras are designed as so-called "waist-level" cameras, with a chimney-style focusing hood into which you peer from above. This standard viewfinder provides a laterally reversed, upright viewing image that is nearly impossible to use with moving subjects but presents few problems with static shots. Only two current medium-format SLR's are designed

Most roll-film SLR's are equipped with an interchangeable waist-level finder as standard, which shows a laterally reversed image. This Hasselblad 500C/M 6 X 6 cm SLR has an eye-level prism finder instead of waist-level unit. Prism finder shows upright, laterally correct image, and is more convenient for following active subjects. Courtesy Braun North America.

like oversized 35 mm SLR's and are obviously intended for eye-level operation. All the cameras in this category accept interchangeable viewfinders, and eye-level pentaprisms are popular as a replacement for the standard hood. Some also feature user-interchangeable focusing screens.

An accessory that is often purchased shortly after the pentaprism is a pistol grip or other type of hand grip to help hold the camera at eye level. Most users find that the basic box shape of cameras designed to be looked down into is rather awkward to hold at eye level without a secure hand grip.

SHUTTERS

Some roll-film SLR's have mechanical or electronically timed focal-plane shutters, with top speeds generally of 1/1000 sec. Others use between-the-lens leaf shutters with top speeds in the range of 1/400 to 1/500 sec. Several models have a focal-plane shutter built into the camera body and can also accept interchangeable lenses equipped with between-the-lens leaf shutters. The focal-plane-shutter models have the edge in lens interchangeability, as it is often possible to adapt special-purpose lenses made by other manufacturers to fit them. The models that rely on between-the-lens leaf shutters built into each interchangeable lens are usually limited to lenses available from the camera manufacturers, as adaptation of other lenses when it is possible tends to be very expensive. On the other hand, the leaf-

Resembling oversized 35 mm SLR, Pentax 6X7 with pentaprism is eye-level, focal-plane-shutter SLR that makes ten 2¼" X 2¾" exposures per 120 roll, or 21 per 220 roll. System includes interchangeable lenses, finders, close-up accessories, and hand grips. Courtesy Pentax Corporation.

shutter models offer the greater versatility in working with electronic flash. Cameras that combine a focal-plane shutter with the ability to accept leaf-shutter lenses as well provide maximum versatility, but at a price.

LENSES

For the most part, medium-format SLR's offer substantially similar features to those found on 35 mm SLR's. An important exception exists in regard to lens systems, however. The lens families available for medium-format single-lens reflexes are less extensive than those for 35 mm SLR's. Fewer "exotic" lenses and truly extreme optics are made for roll-film SLR's, and few independent lens manufacturers bother to fill the gaps for an essentially limited market. Maximum lens apertures for medium-format cameras seldom exceed *f*/2.8, and are often smaller. The sheer size of the elements required for faster lenses would be prohibitive in cost and practical usability. As a class, medium-format SLR's are not well suited to low-light photography, unless circumstances permit using quite long exposures.

OTHER FEATURES

An advantage shared by several medium-format SLR's is their use of *interchangeable film magazines*. The magazines hold the film, and are in turn secured to the camera body. With most magazine systems, you have the option of reloading the camera either by reloading the magazine on the camera with a fresh roll of film, or removing the magazine and replacing it with another. Most removable magazines are equipped with dark slides that prevent fogging unexposed film. This allows changing magazines in mid-roll, which is convenient if you wish to use several different kinds of film in random sequence, such as switching from black-and-white to color or from low-speed to high-speed film according to what's best for a given situation. Each magazine of this type has its own film counter, so you can keep track of how many exposures remain. Removable magazines also offer the flexibility of changing format to some extent. A 6 × 6 cm SLR, for example, may be accessorized via interchangeable magazines to produce 4.5 × 6 cm frames, 4 × 4 cm Super Slides, or 6 × 6 cm frames on long rolls of 70 mm perforated film, depending on the magazine selected. The negative aspects of interchangeable film magazines are high initial cost per magazine and the comparatively great bulk and weight compared to a bare roll of film. In practice, many photographers who own interchangeable-magazine cameras live happily with the one film back that came with it when purchased.

Some roll-film SLR's provide accessory magazine inserts in addition to or instead of completely interchangeable magazines. The insert, which fits into the magazine, is the actual holding device for an unexposed roll of film and a take-up spool. Instead of carrying extra loaded magazines, you can carry less expensive, smaller, and lighter preloaded film inserts, which drop into the magazine shell almost like a film cartridge. You give up the ability to change film in mid-roll, but you get reasonable convenience at a less exorbitant cost.

An outstanding advantage of medium-format SLR's with removable film magazines is that they can accept accessory film backs for Polaroid Land instant-picture film. This allows you to check lighting and composition in an actual photograph made on the spot, with very little delay and no need for processing facilities. To the professional photographer, this capability may be as valuable as all the rest of the camera's features put together. No matter how experienced a photographer may be, there's nothing like having a Polaroid test shot in hand to show beyond doubt that everything looks right from the camera's point of view.

Unlike the 35 mm SLR scene, which is experiencing a proliferation of motorized film winders and electric motor drives, medium-format SLR's are, with few exceptions, manually advanced and cocked. The usual methods are a winding knob or crank at the side of the camera box, or a 35 mm-style thumb lever for eye-level models. The electric-drive exceptions are designed from the beginning as motor-driven cameras, and motor units are built in. In view of the limited film capacity of most medium-format SLR's, extended rapid-fire shooting is not a pressing consideration. Motor-driven medium-format SLR's are most often used simply to relieve the photographer of the distraction of winding the camera between shots when the subject requires undivided attention. Typical situations would include portraiture and fashion or beauty photography, in which fleeting expressions make or break the picture.

As many newer medium-format SLR's produce rectangular 4.5 × 6 cm or 6 × 7 cm frames, it's worth noting that those designed initially for waist-level viewing tend to be awkward to use for vertical pictures, even when equipped with an optional pentaprism finder, with one notable exception. The Mamiya RB67 Pro-S permits orienting the removable film back for horizontal or vertical framing without changing the position of the camera body proper. The catch is that the ground glass shows the equivalent of a square 7 × 7 cm image, with indicators to remind you whether to compose for a horizontal or vertical 6 × 7 cm frame within the overall area. If you're not careful, you may discover too late that you ignored the indicators and have been shooting verticals with the magazine oriented for horizontals, or vice versa.

Except for the few models designed specifically as eye-level cameras, most medium-format SLR's are at their best when used on a tripod or at least under fairly controlled conditions that give the photographer a chance to work deliberately. Unless you have the physique and stamina of King Kong, you'll be inviting collapse if you try to lug around a 35 mm-style assortment of one or two camera bodies and three or four interchangeable lenses for your medium-format SLR outfit.

In keeping with the sizable mechanisms and large reflex mirrors used in roll-film SLR's, these cameras tend to be fairly noisy and generate noticeable vibration when fired. Forget about using them in any situation where extraneous sounds are frowned on, such as concert halls and TV, film, or recording studios. If you expect to do much close-up work or photography with long lenses, make sure any camera you select has a manual mirror release or mirror lock to help reduce vibration immediately before the exposure. As a rule to which there may be exceptions, large focal-plane shutters tend to produce more vibration than leaf shutters.

On balance, the medium-format SLR is a valuable working tool for the professional photographer who needs a larger film original than he can get with 35 mm, but who does not need the film size or corrective capabilities obtained with sheet-film cameras. In this context, the roll-film SLR fills the gap, with significantly more film area than the smaller cameras, and much less cumbersome operation than the larger cameras. For general photography, however, the 35 mm SLR's and rangefinder cameras are far more adaptable to a variety of applications and are much easier to handle.

11

Twin-Lens Reflex Cameras

Twin-lens reflex cameras in roll-film sizes used to be very popular because they offered useful compromises to photographers seeking good image quality without the picture-taking constraints imposed by large-format cameras. TLR's provided ground-glass viewing and focusing, fairly fast hand-held operation, and a decent-size medium-format image for good enlargeability even with the relatively grainy, not-so-sharp films of the period. Until the end of the 1940's the fine 35 mm cameras available didn't seriously rival the TLR, even though they were certainly more convenient. At the other end of the size spectrum, large-format sheet-film cameras offered little competition, too. They yielded beautifully enlargeable negatives, but were heavy, slow to operate, and often required the use of a tripod. Today the situation has changed greatly.

Films have improved to the point that for many applications, enlargements from 35 mm are more than adequate, and are sometimes preferable to results obtained with roll film. In shooting color transparencies, for example, 35 mm Kodachrome films, which are virtually grainless and exquisitely sharp, often reproduce better than roll-film transparencies shot on other types of color material, despite the size advantage of the roll formats.

Both 35 mm and roll-film SLR cameras now offer convenience and versatility that far outstrip the potential of the TLR. And the need for large-format photography is now often based more on the unique capabilities of large-format cameras rather than on a specific need for large film, although there are still occasions when there is simply no substitute for square inches.

All things considered, there is comparatively little need—

With relatively static subjects, waist-level TLR viewing poses no problem. It is very convenient for photographing from low camera position. Good-size negative allows enlarging portion of image as a poor man's telephoto.

or demand—for twin-lens reflex cameras. Nonetheless, the TLR is still a viable camera for general photography, and should not be written off too quickly.

FORMATS

Current twin-lens reflex cameras span a range of formats from 14 × 21 mm to 5″ × 7″, with the most common format being 6 × 6 cm on 120 or 220 roll film. All the TLR's are designed basically as look-down-into cameras, but most can be fitted with optional eye-level pentaprism finders. Looking down at the ground-glass screen through the standard finder shows an upright, laterally reversed viewing/focusing image. Because the image is laterally reversed, it is difficult to track moving subjects. Unfortunately, the shape of most TLR's is such that they are awkward to use at eye level. Many photographers who add a pentaprism wind up adding a pistol grip or other accessory hand grip to make the unit more manageable. An unaccessorized medium-format TLR is about the size and weight of an average-size 35 mm SLR. With added pentaprism and hand grip, it becomes considerably bulkier and heavier.

LENSES

Traditional roll-film TLR's are equipped with noninterchangeable lenses of normal focal length. Mamiya, however, produces several model variations of a roll-film TLR that accepts interchangeable lens panels with matched taking and viewing

Waist-level focusing hood is standard finder of Rolleiflex 3.5F and other medium-format twin-lens reflex cameras. Other interchangeable finders are available for Rollei and some other TLR's. A strong point of TLR's generally is comparative simplicity, ruggedness, and dependability. Courtesy EPOI.

lenses in a variety of focal lengths. An unusual series of large-format sheet-film TLR's bearing the Gowlandflex brand name also offers a degree of lens interchangeability. They are available for 4″ × 5″ and 5″ × 7″ sheet film. As each interchangeable lens for a TLR is actually an assembly consisting of two lenses, size, weight, and cost may be appreciable.

SHUTTERS

Shutters in current TLR's are usually between-the-lens leaf types with speeds ranging from approximately one second to a top of 1/400 or 1/500 sec. Nearly all are extremely quiet, and are therefore unlikely to distract or annoy subjects or bystanders. As with leaf shutters generally, electronic flash synchronization is possible at most or all shutter speeds, providing excellent versatility for flash photography.

FILM ADVANCE

Among roll-film TLR's, film advance and shutter cocking are simultaneous, via a crank on the right side. Unfortunately from the standpoint of convenient operation, several TLR's focus via a wheel on the left side of the camera. Using one of these models hand-held involves shifting the camera back and forth

Unlike other roll-film TLR's, Mamiya models feature interchangeable lenses. Matched taking and viewing lenses are mounted on lens board that clamps in position on camera's front standard. On Mamiya C330F shown, shiny lens-retaining clamps are visible just above viewing lens and below taking lens. Courtesy Bell & Howell/Mamiya Company.

Although TLR's are inherently less versatile than SLR's, some can be accessorized to handle a wide range of situations. Accessories for Rolleiflex TLR's include underwater housing, rigid chimney-type finder, pentaprism finder, pistol grip, and 35 mm film adapter kit, among others. Courtesy EPOI.

from hand to hand depending on whether you're advancing film or focusing. Multiple exposures may be made easily with the large-format TLR's because shutter cocking is independent of film changing. Many medium-format TLR's of recent vintage have multiple-exposure controls for disengaging the film transport from the shutter-cocking mechanism. Older models generally lack this feature.

PARALLAX CORRECTION

Most higher-quality, recent-model TLR's provide automatic parallax correction if they focus close enough to require it. Because of the separation between the viewing and taking lens, TLR's are not well suited to close-up photography, although considerable ingenuity has been expended on producing a variety of accessories designed to circumvent this basic fact. Even with a bag full of expensive close-up accessories and parallax-compensating gadgets, the TLR remains an inefficient close-up camera, despite occasional pieces of manufacturers' literature that might lead you to think otherwise.

VIEWING/FOCUSING

Most TLR focusing screens are not interchangeable by the user. However, if you find you like everything about a particular model except the focusing screen, you may be able to have it changed for another type by the manufacturer's or importer's service department or an independent service facility. The replacement screen may come from another model within the brand, from another manufacturer altogether, or may be custom-made to suit your taste.

Tiny Tessina 35L TLR makes up to 24 frames measuring 14 × 21 mm on a strip of user-respooled 35 mm film. This model also has integral spring-motor film advance for single-frame or sequence shooting, and coupled light meter. Accessories include interchangeable finders. Courtesy Karl Heitz, Inc.

FILMS

Recent medium-format TLR's accept both 120 and 220 film. Older models generally accept only 120. If you're looking at older used cameras, you may also run across TLR's that make 4 × 4 cm pictures on 127 roll film.

A family of unusually small TLR's is made by Tessina, a Swiss company. The Tessinas use 35 mm film loaded into special Tessina magazines to produce up to 24 frames measuring 14 × 21 mm. Features of various models include a built-in spring-motor film advance and a selenium-cell light meter. The cameras are small enough to wear on a wristband, like a bloated watch, and weigh just a few ounces. They are precisely made and are expensive. Tessinas are probably excellent choices for surreptitious photography.

EXPOSURE METERS

Light meters, when built into TLR's, are simply small exposure meters with a selenium or CdS cell aimed toward the area in front of the lens. More elaborate meters that read through the camera's viewing lens may be built into optional pentaprism finders. With noninterchangeable-lens TLR's, through-the-lens metering provides little advantage other than eye-level exposure control. With interchangeable-lens models, through-the-lens metering may be expected to produce more accurate exposures when wide-angle or telephoto lenses are used, as compared with readings that do not take into account the actual field that is being photographed.

Probably the greatest virtue of good-quality TLR's is that they are rugged, dependable cameras. They are much less complex internally than SLR's, so are more likely to survive minor mishaps. If your projected use of a camera is such that its survivability counts for more than its versatility, you should seriously consider using a TLR.

12

Sheet-Film Cameras

Large-format sheet-film cameras have been part of photography in one form or another since photography's earliest days, and they are still going strong. They owe their continued existence to the simple fact that the more square inches of image area in the camera original, the higher the technical quality of the final picture, all other factors being equal. Also, certain large-format cameras provide remarkable control possibilities for manipulating the image. There are four basic types of large-format sheet-film cameras: view cameras, portrait cameras, press cameras, and field cameras. In some respects their capabilities overlap; in others they are quite distinct.

VIEW CAMERAS

At first glance, the view camera looks deceptively simple. A lens standard at the front accepts almost any lens you can physically fit into an appropriately sized lens board, which locks into a recess in the standard. A ground-glass screen at the rear of the camera presents an inverted, laterally reversed image of the subject as formed by the lens. The ground-glass screen is mounted in a frame on the rear standard. The frame may be moved away from the standard against spring tension to permit insertion of a film holder, which is clamped securely between the ground-glass frame and the rear standard. The front and the rear standards are connected by a collapsible, accordion-like bellows, which forms a flexible, lighttight chamber between the standards. The front and rear standards are mounted in alignment on a single metal rail called a monorail, or on a set of parallel rails mounted on a long, flat bed. Both standards can move forward

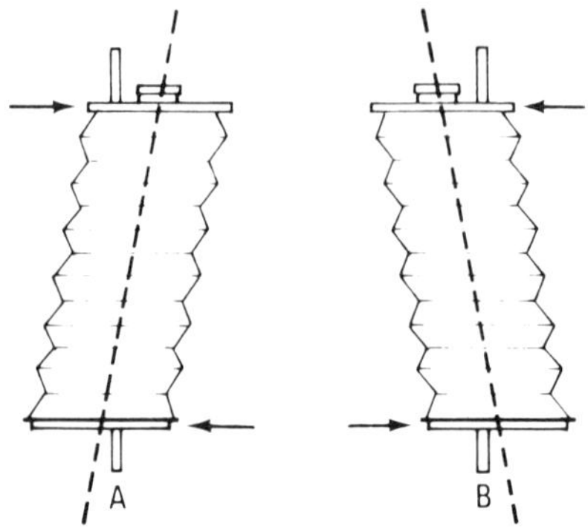

Shifts

Shifts are lateral displacements of view camera's front and rear standards relative to center line of camera's bed or monorail. Front standard of camera (A) is shifted right, rear standard is shifted left. Camera (B) displays opposite shifts. Dashed lines indicate that each camera will photograph obliquely with respect to lens axis.

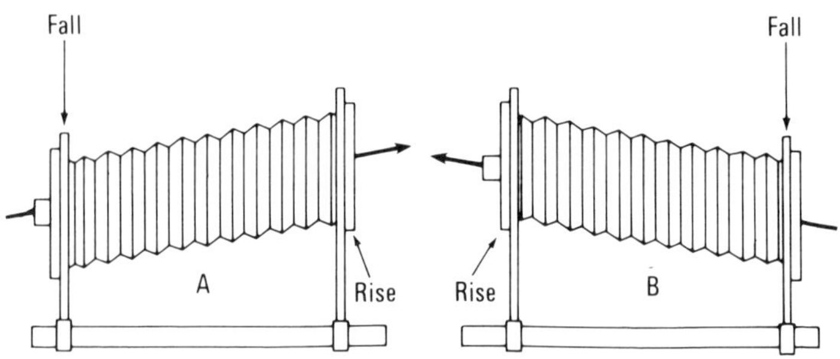

Rises and falls

Rises and falls are, respectively, upward and downward sliding movements of view camera's front and rear standards. Dashed lines indicate that camera (A) will photograph downward and camera (B) will photograph upward although lens and film standards remain perfectly vertical. With movements shown, camera (B) might photograph a tall building without any keystoning of image.

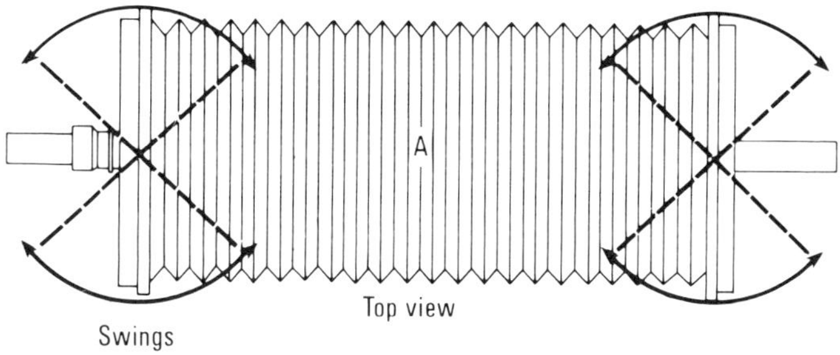

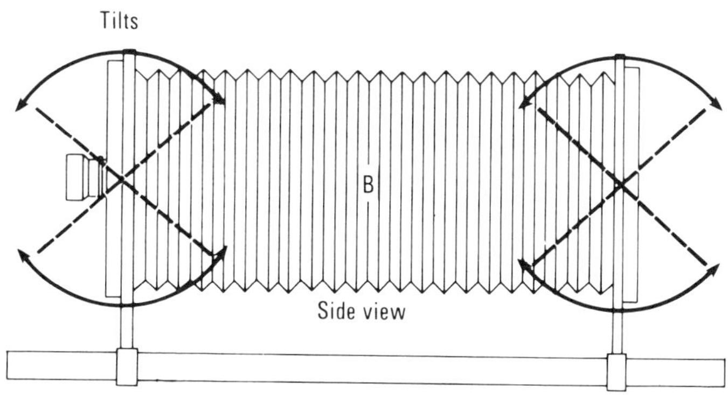

Swings (A) are pivoting movements of a view camera's front and rear standards about a vertical axis. Tilts (B) are pivoting movements of standards about horizontal axis. Central swing and tilt axes, as shown, are common, but some cameras have eccentrically pivoted swings and tilts. Front swings and tilts control placement of sharp zone in image. Rear swings and tilts control perspective.

Practical use of shifts solves problem of photographing front of house when hedge is in way. Shifting lens board left and film back right allows shooting to left along dashed line, while lens and film look straight ahead. Resulting photo will show rectilinear perspective of front of house, as though photographed from front and center.

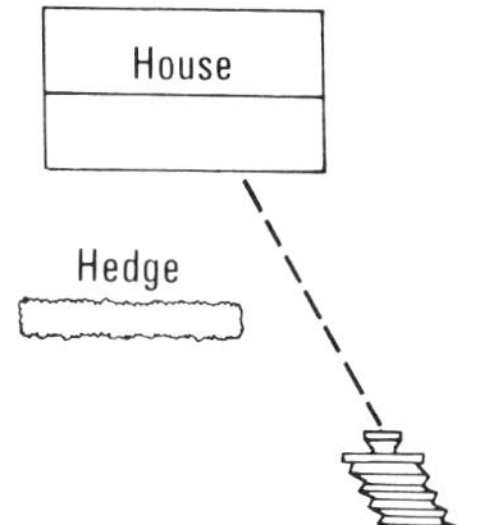

Modular monorail design of Linhof Kardan B view camera and extensive accessory system enhance its versatility. It is available in versions for 4″ × 5″, 5″ × 7″, and 8″ × 10″ sheet films. Each version may be converted to use other sizes. For photographers obsessed with image quality, view cameras are a turn-on. Courtesy H.P. Marketing Corp.

and backward on the monorail or flat bed. This permits focusing a wide range of lens focal lengths. The monorail or flat bed is normally equipped with a block underneath for mounting on a tripod. Often, the monorail or bed may be moved back and forth relative to the mounting block. This is useful for balancing the camera on the block as well as for focusing by moving the entire camera closer to or farther from a small close-up subject without having to shift the tripod. Many view cameras are equipped with one or more bubble levels to help true up the camera and to check positioning of movable components.

CAMERA MOVEMENTS

Besides fore and aft focusing movements, the front and rear standards can also move horizontally and vertically. Displacements of the lens or film standard to the left or right of center are called *shifts*. Raising and lowering movements are referred to in terms of *rising* and *falling*, respectively. These vertical and lateral movements allow considerable latitude in positioning the image within the film format without actually having to change the aiming point of the camera itself. For example, raising the lens and/or dropping the camera back allow the view camera to photograph "uphill" to include the top of a tall building within the frame. Yet the camera can remain level, with the film parallel to the building's vertical axis, so the vertical lines of the building are rendered parallel on film. Horizontal shifts allow considerable freedom to photograph obliquely without foregoing the familiar and easily accepted perspective associated with "head-on" camera placement. This capability is important to architectural photographers, who must often photograph building facades with four-square rectilinearity, even though terrain features or other obstacles prevent positioning the camera front and center. The practical advantages of using rises, falls, and horizontal shifts are too numerous to catalog, but one more example may further whet your curiosity. Judicious use of these movements makes it possible to pull off visual tricks such as photographing a room interior that includes a large mirror that appears to be facing squarely into the camera lens, yet no reflection of the camera is seen. In this case, the camera movements avoid considerable costly after-the-fact retouching.

Other movement capabilities of view cameras are the *tilts* and *swings*. Tilts are forward and backward rotations of the lens standard and rear standard. Depending on the design of the camera, the axis of rotation may be at the center of the lens board or film back, at or near the base, or at the attachment point where the standard meets the monorail or flat bed. Swings are left and right pivoting movements of the lens standard and rear standard. As with tilts, swing axes may be central or off center, depending on specific camera design. As a rule, central swing and tilt axes are the easiest to learn to use. Experienced view-camera users sometimes prefer eccentrically pivoted swings and tilts because they can be more extreme in the range of movement, and, according to manufacturers of such cameras, may offer other advantages as well.

In practice, swinging and tilting the lens standard are considered controls over the distribution of depth of field in the photograph. Swinging and tilting the rear standard are considered determinants of perspective. Although these statements are true, one occasionally runs into gray areas of overlapping utility. In any case, it isn't a problem because you can see exactly what's happening to the image on the ground glass.

The swinging and tilting lens movements provide amazing

flexibility in "warping" the plane of maximum sharpness forward and back and from side to side. Although all photographers using view cameras find this facility useful, it is most appreciated by still-life photographers and others who are routinely faced with the problem of attempting to show subjects clearly in depth at close working distances. The view camera's front swings and tilts allow twisting the plane of sharpness in complex ways that are not easily described.

Swings and tilts of the rear standard are customarily used to position the film plane relative to the subject so that the appearance of the subject in the picture suits the photographer's needs and/or tastes. Depending on how the photographer uses the rear swings and tilts, he may produce a realistic, literal-looking rendition of the subject, or a deliberately elongated, foreshortened, or otherwise distorted version. The effects can be dramatic or subtle, attractive or unattractive, truthful or deceitful.

Although the preceding discussion of view-camera movements treats them individually, a photographer adjusting a view camera for a specific photograph may at some point use any or all

View-camera movements provide precise control of perspective and distribution of sharpness in picture, and large film formats can render subject tones and textures as photographer wishes. View cameras and sheet film are top choice for making still lifes.

simultaneously. To the bystander, the camera may appear contorted beyond practical use.

Because standard sheet-film formats are rectangular, view cameras are designed either with rotating film backs or with film backs that may be removed and repositioned for shooting horizontal or vertical subjects. Because of constraints imposed by camera size, rotating backs are more likely to be found on 4″ × 5″ view cameras than on larger sizes.

Not all view cameras provide all the movements described, nor are they all equal in the degree of movements provided or the convenience with which adjustments may be made. As a rule, the more expensive and more elaborate the camera, the more movements and the greater the range of any given movement. The exception to the rule concerns camera size. The larger the film format, the more the camera is likely to cost, and the more limited the range of movements.

Convenience of adjusting movements varies a great deal. For example, some view cameras use a separate lock for every movement. This may slow you down when you want to make major, sweeping changes in the camera set-up, but it protects you from accidentally loosening an intricate combination of adjustments. Another camera may use one lock to control several adjustments. If you're adept with a view camera, such a system allows very fast, easy adjusting. If you're not sure of yourself, though, trying to handle more than one adjustment at a time may be disconcerting.

LENSES AND SHUTTERS

New view-camera lenses tend to be very expensive, so, again, it may be worth your while to shop for a good used lens. Most lenses for view cameras are mounted with their own between-the-lens shutters, as view cameras are not designed with integral shutters. A few of the modular-system view cameras offer optional camera-mounted shutter units that eliminate the need for individual lens-shutters. These shutter units are very expensive initially, but may save a photographer money in the long run by letting him acquire barrel-mounted lenses, which do not have expensive built-in individual shutters. Unless you expect to collect a wide range of lenses, the economy aspect may be illusory. Some photographers, though, prefer to work with an integral shutter unit because of the greater exposure consistency achieved by using only one shutter rather than several.

The shutters provided for view-camera lenses are leaf-type models. Top speeds are in the area of 1/400 or 1/500 sec. in small-size shutters and about 1/125 sec. or slower in large-size shutters. Most are mechanically timed, but some electronically timed view-camera shutters are available.

In view of the considerable displacement of the film relative to the lens axis that can occur when using even moderate swings, tilts, shifts, rises, and falls, singly or in combination, a versatile view-camera lens must provide a much larger image circle than is necessary simply to contain the diagonal of the film format. The "excess" coverage when the camera is "zeroed" with no movements in use quickly becomes vital as adjustments move the center of the film outward relative to the center of the image circle. Therefore, a key specification to weigh when comparing view-camera lenses is the actual diameter of the image circle. Manufacturers of view-camera lenses often publish image-circle figures for the lenses they produce. The data may be available for the lens at maximum aperture and stopped down (the usable image circle frequently increases as the lens is stopped down). The larger the image circle relative to the diagonal of the film, the more leeway you have to use the movements the camera provides. When the image circle is too small, you may find that even modest camera adjustments bring corners or edges of the

Full view-camera movements can be used only with lenses that project large image circles. Small image circle (A) that just covers format when no movements are used fills barely half frame with full rise and shift movements (dashed outlines). Large image circle (B) permits use of extreme shifts. Portrait lenses may have small image circles, as major camera movements are not anticipated in portraiture.

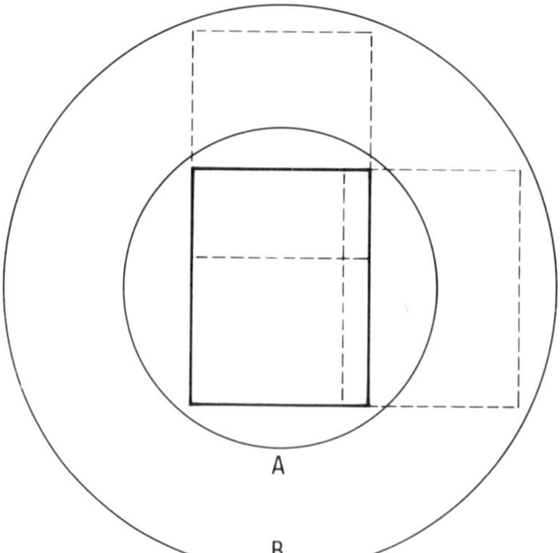

film into fringe areas of coverage that produce a degraded, mushy-looking image. In extreme cases, portions of the film may lie completely beyond the image circle, and be unexposed. You can see this happening on the ground glass, of course, but that's small consolation.

Not all lenses designed for large-format photography have large image circles. Portrait lenses and process lenses, to name just two categories, are seldom designed with large-image circles, because it is assumed that neither portraiture nor reprographic work requires more than minimal use of camera movements. The same often applies to the longer telephoto lenses.

FORMATS

For general use, the 4″ × 5″ format makes the most sense, particularly if you are new to view-camera photography. It's large enough to produce superb enlargements, yet the film is not difficult to handle nor is it inhibitingly expensive. There is a wide variety of view cameras available in 4″ × 5″.

A particularly strong argument in favor of the 4″ × 5″ view camera is the availability of a selection of excellent 4″ × 5″ Polaroid Land films and an easy-to-use holder for them.

View cameras for 5″ × 7″ and 8″ × 10″ film are necessarily much larger and heavier than 4″ × 5″ models. Consequently, they are more difficult to handle both in terms of in-studio set-up and location travel. This applies not only to the basic camera, but also to accessories, lenses, and film holders. Most photographers who work with view cameras larger than 4″ × 5″ do so because they absolutely need the additional square inches of film. If a highly detailed subject must be recorded with maximum clarity and impeccable tone reproduction, it's hard to ignore the advantage of using 80 square inches of film to do the job in preference to 20. Typical uses of 8″ × 10″ view cameras include making color copies of paintings for reproduction in high-quality art books, commercial still-life photography, and shooting color originals for enlargement to poster or billboard sizes. These are applications in which there is simply no substitute for the additional film area.

As a rule, 8″ × 10″ view cameras provide fewer and less extreme adjustments than their 4″ × 5″ counterparts. The size of the mechanical components found on 8″ × 10″ cameras is such that it is sometimes not practical to build-in the extra space to accommodate certain movements, because the over-all structure would become almost unusably large.

Many 8″ × 10″ and 5″ × 7″ view cameras can be adapted to use 4″ × 5″ film for jobs that don't require the larger sizes. The smaller film is much less expensive per sheet, and processing costs are correspondingly lower, too. Fitting a 4″ × 5″ back on a larger camera also permits use of Polaroid Land film for test shooting, even though the test shot will represent only a

Ground-glass viewing/focusing screen of view camera shows image upside down and laterally reversed.

To eliminate inconvenience of viewing inverted, reversed image under focusing cloth, a variety of accessory focusing devices is available for some view cameras. Binocular reflex magnifier fitted to Sinar-f camera has reflex mirror that presents upright focusing image, which binocular eyepiece magnifies for accurate focusing. Courtesy EPOI.

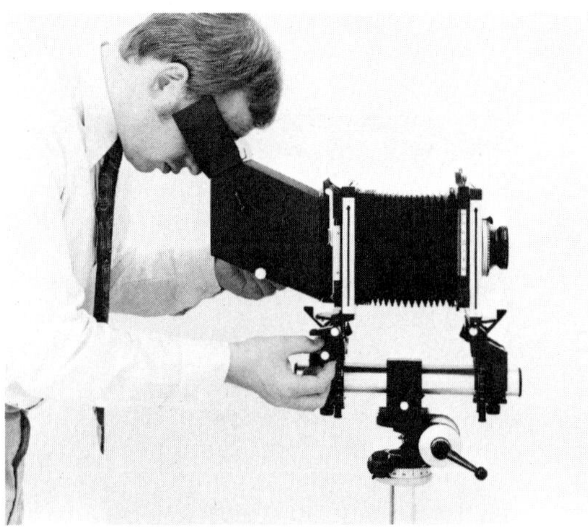

section of the larger format. In many situations, a test shot of a section of the scene is preferable to no test shot at all. (Although 8″ × 10″ Polaroid Land color film is available, it is rather expensive for test-shot use.)

At the opposite end of the view-camera size scale, some models are available for 2¼″ × 3¼″ sheet film. These cameras are smaller and lighter, and so are their lenses, accessories, and film holders. They may be useful for location shooting that requires view-camera movements, but not necessarily a large sheet of film.

ACCESSORIES

In addition to their built-in versatility, some view cameras, particularly all-metal monorail types, may be accessorized almost beyond recognition. Extra lengths of monorail, add-on bellows sections, and additional bellows supports permit extending the camera dramatically for close-up photography. Interchangeable front and rear standards and bellows sections can let you make 4″ × 5″ pictures in the morning and 8″ × 10″ pictures later in

Upright buildings and the tonal quality of large film are ample incentives to put up with the real bother of hauling view camera, tripod, film holders, and accessories on location.

the day with the same basic camera. Instead of using a black focusing cloth, you may find a rigid accessory focusing hood with built-in critical magnifier more to your taste. One manufacturer even lists hardware for mounting a second complete view camera piggyback atop the one that's being used to make the picture. The top camera is supposed to function as an optical viewfinder, apparently, while the film holder prevents viewing through the bottom camera. About the only accessory you can't find for view cameras is a motor drive.

THE CASE FOR USED VIEW CAMERAS

If you're thinking of buying a view camera, consider the following points: View cameras have been around a long time, during which they have not changed much from a functional standpoint. A modern view camera may be precisely machined of gleaming alloys while its ancestor was precisely handcrafted of selected hardwoods, but they share the same movements and general capabilities. You may save quite a lot of money by shopping around for a good used older view camera, and not give up much in the way of performance. True, many modern machines are capable of more extreme adjustments than older view cameras, but for most purposes extreme adjustments aren't necessary. Furthermore, several current view cameras are capable of dramatic contortions that are photographically useless, because available lenses are unable to provide a large enough image circle to cover the film format when the extreme adjustments are employed. The comfort of knowing that the camera provides more extreme movements than you can possibly use is costly.

If you prefer investing in a new camera but wish to economize, several manufacturers make basic models that are eminently usable. As with vintage view cameras, they may offer more limited movements than the expensive models, but are still excellent learning devices and more than satisfactory for day-to-day professional studio use. Most of the basic models cannot be accessorized and adapted anywhere near as extensively as the high-priced modular view cameras. However, this is not much of a drawback for nonspecialized large-format photography.

STUDIO PORTRAIT CAMERAS

Studio portrait cameras are quite similar to view cameras, except they lack some view-camera movements. They have been made in most large-format sizes, and as with many view cameras, adapters are often available for downsizing larger models to

This portrait photographer in early 1880's must have been proud of his newfangled electric floodlight. Even so, the sitter required a neck brace to hold long pose with slow films of the day. One thing that hasn't changed appreciably is the classic sheet-film portrait camera. Such cameras are still encountered in studios oriented toward traditional, formal portraiture. Courtesy New York Public Library Picture Collection.

accept smaller film. They are an obsolescent breed of camera, as public taste is shifting from formal studio portraiture to informal images better made with smaller cameras.

As portrait cameras are not called on to photograph oddly shaped objects from unusual angles, they do not need the wide range of adjustments normally built into view cameras. Most portrait cameras provide front rises and falls for positioning the image vertically in the frame without tilting the whole camera, or changing its elevation relative to the subject. Some also provide limited front swings and tilts to help place the zone of sharpness in best relationship to the subject. This is sometimes necessary in lieu of closing down the lens diaphragm to gain depth of field, because many soft-focus portrait lenses lose their appealing softness when used at small apertures. The rear standards of portrait cameras often provide no adjustments.

Portrait cameras are generally of flat-bed design, and quite solidly made. Light weight is not a factor, as the cameras are intended for studio use exclusively. As single-purpose instru-

Soft-focus portrait lenses or diffusion devices that soften images made with inherently sharp lenses are advisable when photographing women's faces at close range. Even superb complexion benefits from a touch of diffusion when face will fill or overflow frame.

ments, they are seldom capable of being accessorized into anything other than what they are.

Lenses for portrait cameras interchange via lens boards, as is the case with view cameras. Although any lens of appropriate focal length and covering power may be used, traditional portrait photographers often employ lenses designed specifically to soften the image.

Press cameras are folding, flat-bed sheet-film cameras with coupled rangefinders and optical viewfinders. Built-in ground-glass panels and view camera movements allow some to handle typical view-camera situations. Linhof Super Technika V uses 2¼" X 3¼" sheet film and is among the most versatile, with broad range of movements and accessories. Linhof and other press cameras are also made for 4" X 5" film. Courtesy H.P. Marketing Corp.

PRESS CAMERAS

Press cameras are the opposite sheet-film extreme relative to portrait cameras. Although few press photographers now use them, hand-held, flat-bed folding 4" × 5" and 2¼" × 3¼" sheet-film cameras were once symbols of news photography. They have survived the trend to smaller cameras because they offer the only practical means of making large-format originals in situations that do not permit setting up a camera on a tripod and proceeding with due deliberation.

Modern press cameras accept conventional sheet-film holders, and have a ground-glass focusing screen for close-up work and other applications involving the use of a tripod. Normally, in hand-held shooting, a large coupled rangefinder is used for focusing, and an optical finder or wire-frame sports finder is used for composing. Press-camera lenses interchange via lens boards, and must be coupled by cam to the camera's rangefinder if rangefinder focusing is desired. Special-purpose lenses that are not rangefinder-coupled may be focused by estimation with reference to an appropriate footage scale, or with the camera's ground glass. Each lens carries its own between-the-lens leaf shutter. (A few vintage press cameras had built-in focal-plane shutters.) Interchangeable lenses with rangefinder coupling cams are generally available in a range from moderate wide-angle to moderate telephoto. However, when rangefinder focusing is not necessary, any lens that can be made to fit the camera's front standard may be used, provided the focusing bellows is long enough to permit focusing at the desired distances.

Lenses designed specifically for press cameras differ somewhat from view-camera lenses because it is assumed that they will not be called on to serve the same functions. A key difference is that press-camera lenses normally have much less covering power than view-camera lenses made for the same format. Although many press cameras provide a few view-camera movements of limited range for occasional use, these movements are not utilized in hand-held photography. Therefore, the basic lenses used for hand-held shooting do not have to project an image circle larger than whatever is needed to cover the film diagonal adequately. As a practical consequence, the lenses can be made somewhat smaller and lighter than their view-camera counterparts, and less expensively. When the photographer expects to use the camera movements for a particular assignment, he leaves the press lenses at home and takes view-camera lenses instead, for their greater covering power.

Most press cameras will accept roll-film adapters for 120/220 film, and Polaroid Land sheet-film or pack-film holders. The roll-film adapters speed up camera operation and reduce the cost per exposure compared with sheet film. Exposing Polaroid materials is as useful to press-camera users as to other photographers.

Although press cameras are no lightweights compared to medium-format and small-format cameras, they are efficient hand-held cameras and are smaller and lighter than view cameras. They let a photographer work fairly freely and quickly without abandoning the qualitative edge of large-format sheet film, and they are reasonably versatile. If you need one, don't be discouraged by the rather high cost of the current surviving models. Press cameras are basically rugged, simple devices, and they haven't changed enough to notice for decades, which means you may find a good, serviceable used press camera for a fraction of what a new one costs, even if you tack on the cost of minor touching up and tightening here and there. The same applies, incidentally, to other large-format cameras. A structurally sound

Field cameras are lightweight view cameras that fold for easy carrying. Movements and focusing travel are often less extreme than with studio view cameras. This Wista "45" 4″ × 5″ camera weighs only 3¼ pounds and measures just 3½″ × 7¼″ × 8½″ folded. Courtesy Foto-Care Limited.

old model can usually do everything the new version can, although it may do so a trifle less conveniently. The money you save may far outweigh the inconvenience.

FIELD CAMERAS

Field cameras are what you get if you combine a view camera and a press camera. The result resembles a compact, flatbed folding view camera, or a press camera stripped of its rangefinder/viewfinder system. They are designed for portability in the field, but they are definitely tripod cameras and not equipped for hand-held shooting. Most field cameras are made for 4″ × 5″ film, but smaller sizes and larger formats up to 8″ × 10″ are available, both new and used.

To reduce weight and bulk, some features have been

omitted. Generally, field cameras provide fewer and less extreme movements than full-fledged view cameras, but more than a press camera normally provides. Accessory systems for field cameras are much less extensive than those for view cameras. And most field cameras are not designed in modular fashion to permit switching components such as shorter or longer bellows sections. Nonetheless, they manage to provide a large measure of view-camera capability in a somewhat less cumbersome and more portable package. An archeologist on a dig, a landscape photographer, and a fashion photographer making location pictures for a catalog, might each find a large-format field camera the perfect instrument for his purposes.

If you are one of the growing minority of photographic enthusiasts who thrill to the sight of big, beautiful pictures exhibiting exquisite tones and textures and precisely rendered detail, large-format photography may be for you. It is one of the most demanding and most satisfying areas of photography.

13

Special-Purpose Cameras

Properly accessorized, conventional cameras are often able to do a fine job in specialized applications. Nonetheless, there are situations that are best handled with specialized, single-purpose cameras. Although such machines are of little use to the photographic generalist, they may be invaluable to the photographer with a narrowly defined task that cannot be handled efficiently, if at all, with conventional equipment.

There are so many varieties of special-purpose cameras that a comprehensive, in-depth analysis is beyond the scope of this book. However, a brief overview of several categories of specialized equipment is useful to provide at least a hint of what lies beyond the bounds of "normal," everyday photography as practiced by the majority of photographers.

WIDE-ANGLE AND PANORAMIC CAMERAS

Wide-angle and panoramic cameras are both used to make pictures that include more subject matter than usual on film, but they do so in different ways and the resulting pictures are not at all interchangeable in terms of look and "feel."

Wide-angle cameras are made for film sizes from 35 mm through roll film and sheet film. Lenses are generally not interchangeable, and focal lengths normally are very short for the respective film format, with an extremely wide angle of view. Leaf shutters are the rule, although older 35 mm models sometimes have focal-plane shutters. Focusing is normally done by scale, with no built-in focusing aid. Viewing is by optical or wire-frame finder. One or more bubble levels may be attached to the camera body to facilitate precise leveling. Some wide-angle

Special-purpose wide-angle camera, Brooks-Veriwide 100 covers 100° angle of view with 47 mm lens. Interchangeable film backs include 120/220 roll holder (rear) for eight or sixteen $2\frac{1}{4}'' \times 3\frac{1}{4}''$ exposures, and Polaroid pack-film back. Dark slide permits changing loaded magazines without fogging film. Courtesy Burleigh Brooks Optics Inc.

cameras have interchangeable film backs, and most (except for 35 mm models) accept Polaroid Land film backs or holders.

These cameras all provide super-wide-angle pictures with rectilinear perspective. The visual impact of the pictures derives from the unaccustomed combination of extreme wide-angle effect coupled with straight-line rendition. The cameras are easily hand-held, even in sheet-film versions, but a tripod is almost mandatory for accurate leveling. Wide-angle sheet-film cameras are much easier to carry and set up than view cameras, and offer lens focal lengths shorter than can be used on most view cameras. You get extraordinary large-format wide-angle coverage, but you give up the view camera's swings, tilts, and other adjustments.

Panoramic cameras also present an unusually broad view of the world, but instead of confining it to standard negative dimensions, they sweep the image over a longer-than-normal length of film. This is done by swinging the lens during the exposure, so that it pivots laterally, projecting images of different areas of the scene onto a curved strip of film in the camera. The film plane is curved so that each portion of film exposed is the same distance from the rear of the swinging lens as each previously exposed portion. The lens does not have to be of ultra-

Extra-wide-angle cameras are useful when working in confined areas. Here, a Brooks-Veriwide 100 made passenger compartment of a DC-10 appear luxuriously spacious. Courtesy Burleigh Brooks Optics Inc.

wide-angle design, as a major part of its coverage comes from traversing the scene. The result is a wide-format picture that includes a much wider field than we normally see clearly at any given moment.

Panoramic cameras with swinging lenses have been made in both 35 mm and roll-film sizes. A 35 mm model is available that produces individual frames measuring 24 × 59 mm, with a 140° included angle. Focus is adjustable by scale and an optical finder shows approximately what will appear on film. When cameras of this type are leveled carefully, straight horizontal

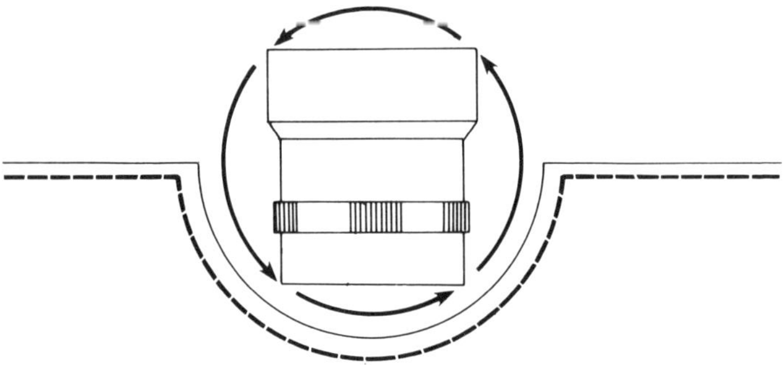

Swinging lens in a panoramic camera pivots during exposure to cover an extremely broad swath of scene. Curved film plane holds film (dashed line) at constant distance relative to rear element of lens. Even if lens is not extreme wide-angle, lateral traverse covers much ground.

lines in the center of the field are rendered as straight. Straight horizontal lines nearer the top or bottom frame edge will appear increasingly bowed as they approach the extreme left and right ends of the frame. When the camera is not leveled, bizarre distortions may be produced. If the camera itself and/or the subject move while the lens is traversing, extreme distortions occur. The effects are difficult to control, but can be graphically interesting when they succeed.

Built-in, battery-powered motor pivots entire Hulcherama Model 120 camera on its mount for 360° panoramic coverage. Manual control permits rotating camera less than or more than 360°. Camera uses conventional 120 or 220 roll film. A 360° picture produces image approximately 2¼" × 9" on film. Courtesy Charles A. Hulcher Co., Inc.

Even more advanced than swing-lens panoramic cameras is a variety capable of making full-circle 360° sweeps. The entire camera pivots on its mounting base, driven by a self-contained motor. Here, too, the moving lens paints the image section-by-section on a curved strip of film, in this case roll film. The speed of rotation and the arc to be covered may be preset. The wide, shallow strip picture that results from 360° coverage can be very disorienting, even when it depicts a basically familiar subject or locale.

Rather than attempt to pinpoint situations where wide-angle and panoramic cameras are useful, consider instead their two strongest attributes: the ability to record a tremendous amount of visual information in coherent relationship, and the potentially strong graphic punch of the pictures. Your needs and creative instincts will tell you everything else you need to know.

RECORDING AND HIGH-SPEED CAMERAS

Recording and high-speed cameras are basically variations on the motor-drive theme. Both types are available for conventional and bulk rolls of 35 mm film, as well as wider-gauge unbacked film in rolls.

Recording cameras are intended primarily for use in fixed installations where repetitive documentation is required. Lenses are interchangeable, to permit covering various fields at suitable distances, but the cameras often lack built-in viewing/focusing systems, which are superfluous once a camera has been set up for a particular job. Motors may be battery- or line-current-powered (some spring-powered models are also made), and tripping may be remotely controlled by a camera operator, intervalometer, or other triggering device. For laboratory or technical recording, many cameras can be tripped conventionally by cable release or shutter-release button. Exposures are normally made one frame at a time rather than in continuous bursts. Depending on the specific application, recording cameras may accept standard film cartridges or special bulk-film backs that permit making as many as 12,000 exposures at one loading. Exposure settings are generally made manually to suit prevailing light levels. Auto-exposure systems are available for installations where the lighting is highly variable.

Typical uses of recording cameras range from taking photomicrographs in pathology labs to monitoring data displays and gauge readings in industry to photographing people in public areas at banks every few seconds. Recording cameras aren't

Recording cameras are used to photograph long series, as in surveillance, instrument monitoring, and process documentation. Robot Motor Recorder uses 35 mm film in long rolls and is electrically driven. Film magazine mounted on camera holds 500 feet producing up to 6,000 24 X 36 mm, 9,000 24 X 24 mm, or 12,000 18 X 24 mm exposures without reloading, depending on format. Smaller magazines hold 30, 100, and 200 feet of film. Courtesy Karl Heitz, Inc.

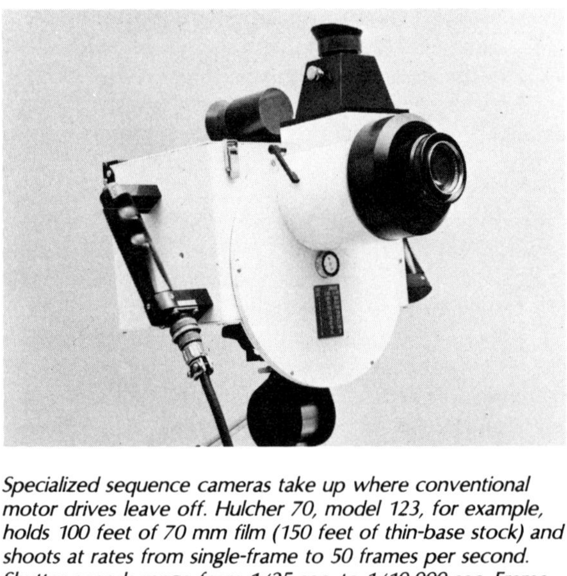

Specialized sequence cameras take up where conventional motor drives leave off. Hulcher 70, model 123, for example, holds 100 feet of 70 mm film (150 feet of thin-base stock) and shoots at rates from single-frame to 50 frames per second. Shutter speeds range from 1/25 sec. to 1/10,000 sec. Frame sizes are 2¼ " X 2¼ " or 2¼ " X 2½ ". Courtesy Charles A Hulcher Co., Inc.

glamorous, but they are functional.

High-speed cameras pick up where conventional motor-drive cameras leave off. Although often made for 35 mm film stock, they may also be found in models for long rolls of film in widths up to 9½ inches or for movie films of various sizes. Framing rates may vary from as slow as an ordinary motor-drive camera to literally thousands of frames per second. It is difficult to describe general characteristics of high-speed cameras because they tend to be highly customized to suit specific customer requirements. Some are battery-operated and relatively portable, and turn up at major sporting events in the hands of photographers seeking dramatic rapid-fire sequences of key game action. Others may be bulky heavyweights installed on huge, high-precision mounts, and used for tracking stages of rocket launchings and suborbital flight. Still other high-speed cameras are used to record shell bursts or catastrophic failures of industrial products undergoing testing. Overall, high-speed cameras give us the opportunity to analyze at leisure events that transpire too quickly to be assimilated any other way.

AERIAL CAMERAS

Logic tells us that any camera at all can be used to photograph the earth from an airplane. Experience, however, dictates that photographers whose livelihoods depend on making good-quality aerial photographs are better off using cameras designed specifically to deliver sharp pictures from hundreds or thousands of feet up.

Hand-held aerial cameras have been made both for conventional film in rolls and sheets and for special aerial films in roll sizes from 70 mm wide and 100 feet long to 9½ inches wide and 2000 feet long. The latter size would certainly be cut into more suitable lengths for hand-held equipment.

Because aerial cameras are used at great distances from the subject, complex viewing and focusing systems are not required. To the extent that focus deviates from infinity, scale adjustment is adequate to cope with it, and most aerial cameras do not provide for close focusing. Viewing is through simple optical or rugged open-frame finders, as hair-splitting framing accuracy is neither necessary nor possible most of the time.

Lenses for aerial cameras are computed specifically for long-distance photography, with optical corrections that may differ considerably from those associated with conventional camera lenses. The corrections that make the lenses brilliant in aerial use may make them unsuitable for closer-range terrestrial

Hand-held aerial cameras are designed to withstand rigors of in-flight photography. Linhof Aero Technika 45 has rigid body, well protected interchangeable lenses, twin contoured hand grips, and makes 4″ × 5″ pictures. Film magazine shown holds about 50 feet of 5″-wide film for 150 exposures. Other backs accept sheet film, medium-format roll film, and Polaroid pack film. Courtesy H.P. Marketing Corp.

applications. Conventional photographic lenses are sometimes used for aerial photography from low altitudes with good results, but higher altitudes do require "aerial lenses" for optimum performance.

Hand-held aerial photography is done through open windows, doors, or special camera ports to achieve best image quality. Since the camera may be subjected to severe wind pressure from slipstream and/or propwash, aerial cameras are solidly built, with rugged attachment points for removable film magazines or accessories. The camera bodies usually have integral hand-grips to facilitate steady holding and to prevent accidental loss over the side. Aerial cameras do not have built-in exposure meters, as exposures are determined according to somewhat different criteria than exposures on the ground.

Although somewhat eclipsed in recent years by the seeming magic of pictures transmitted from satellites or retrieved from space vehicles, aerial photographs taken with hand-held equipment are still being made in large numbers and are likely to continue being made for quite some time. They serve the needs of cartographers, agricultural and wildlife organizations, industry, real estate and municipal groups, news media, and tourist boards, to mention just a few consumers of aerial photos.

UNDERWATER CAMERAS

Although underwater housings can adapt ordinary cameras to undersea use, true underwater cameras represent a more direct approach. Underwater cameras are water-tight, built of corrosion-resistant materials, and equipped with lenses specially computed for photography in water rather than air. Many underwater cameras are one-of-a-kind or limited-production designs developed to satisfy specific underwater shooting requirements. Among the criteria that affect the final "package" are film size, probable working distances from subjects and field sizes to be covered, maximum depths, and need to use auxiliary lighting vs. availability of adequate ambient light.

Among off-the-shelf underwater cameras, the Nikonos is probably the best known and most widely used. It accepts conventional 35 mm cartridges and makes full-size 24 × 36 mm

Water-tight body of Nikonos III 35 mm camera makes underwater photography more convenient by eliminating need for special housing. Professional photographers sometimes use it on land in bad weather or other situations in which a doused camera is likely. Courtesy Nikon Inc. (EPOI).

Scuba diver with Nikonos camera, holding underwater flash unit in left hand. Heavily shielded synchronization cable and connectors are needed to prevent shorts. Courtesy Nikon Inc. (EPOI).

frames. The standard lens is a 35 mm *f*/2.5 that scale-focuses to 31.5 inches, and interchanges with other bayonet-mount lenses with focal lengths ranging from 15 mm to 80 mm. All lenses designed for the Nikonos are computed specifically for underwater use. A built-in optical finder has frame lines for 35 mm and 80 mm fields, and accessory finders are used with other lenses. The camera has a metal focal-plane shutter with speeds from 1/30 to 1/500 sec., plus "B," and has a waterproof synchronization outlet for underwater flash. Accessories for the Nikonos include underwater close-up and flash equipment, an exposure meter, various finders, and filters. The camera is rated for use as deep as 160 feet below the surface, and is impressively rugged. Earlier versions of the camera were sold under the Calypso brand name.

As a point of interest, some news photographers have used Nikonos cameras on land for covering assignments in rain, snow, or other conditions that make camera-drenching likely.

14

Instant-Picture Cameras

In a class by themselves, instant-picture cameras offer snapshot photographers completely automatic operation, drop-in film loading, and, best of all, finished pictures within minutes or seconds of pushing the shutter release, with no separate processing procedure required. Deluxe-model instant-picture cameras are priced as much as ten times higher than basic models, but they all do very much the same job. As a rule, top-price models provide better-quality lenses, more complex SLR or

"The explorer furnished with his photographic apparatus, which is now constructed in such a manner that it can be used with ease in any part of the world brings back with him from his travels documents invaluable, because no one can deny their accuracy."—(Gaston Tissandier, 1876.)

An early approach to instant-picture photography, necessitated by materials then in use, consisted of carrying a darkroom on location with the camera, as shown in this 1876 illustration. Current instant-picture techniques were used to reproduce it here. It was copied on high-contrast Polaroid Land Type 51, 4″ × 5″ sheet film. Courtesy New York Public Library Picture Collection.

High-technology snapshot camera, Polaroid Land SX-70 Alpha 1 has automatic exposure, automatic film advance and ejection of dry, developing color print, SLR viewing and focusing to 10.4 inches, and folding superstructure to reduce bulk. Extremely complex in concept, it is extremely easy to use. Courtesy Polaroid Corporation.

rangefinder focusing systems, focusing to 12 inches or less, and automatic motorized film advance and expulsion of the exposed print. Low-price versions are likely to have simple plastic lenses, optical viewfinders, scale focusing to 3½ feet or so, and manual film advance and removal of the exposed picture. The only difference that is likely to be obvious in the final prints is the close-up capability of some top-line SLR models.

Compared to conventional snapshot cameras, instant-picture models are considerably bulkier and heavier. Because the picture you expose is the picture you get, the camera must be large enough to accommodate snapshot-size film and the relatively long-focal-length standard lenses needed to cover the film format. To minimize bulk, some instant-picture cameras are designed with folding bodies that collapse for more compact carrying.

Consistent with their snapshot-camera predestination, instant cameras do not offer lens interchangeability, nor do they boast extensive multi-purpose accessory systems. All provide for automatic flash photography with multi-bulb expendable flash sources, and some models will also accept compatible electronic flash units.

Automatic-exposure systems are of the programmed type, and manual override is limited to a lighten/darken control for biasing the automatically set exposure. Current models do not permit user selection of shutter speeds and *f*-stops, although several older, discontinued instant-picture cameras did feature manual exposure setting. As used cameras in good condition, they command disproportionately high prices. It's unfortunate that manufacturers of instant-picture cameras apparently find it uneconomical to market even one manually controlled model. Instant-picture photography can be such an efficient and pleasant way to learn photography that it's a pity suitable equipment is not available new from the manufacturers of instant-picture materials.

Ironically, the most interesting variety of films for instant-picture photography is found in Polaroid Corporation's line of eight-shot film packs producing a $3\frac{1}{4}'' \times 4\frac{1}{4}''$ print or print plus reusable negative. Unfortunately, the few current general-purpose Polaroid Land cameras that can accept these film packs cannot begin to exploit the films' capabilities. If you wish to enjoy the best in instant-picture photography, as matters now stand, you will have to expose instant-picture materials in conventional cameras via adapter backs or film holders.

Optical finders with coupled rangefinder device for focusing to $3\frac{1}{2}$ feet are among features of Eastman Kodak's Colorburst 100 and 200 instant snapshot cameras. They automatically eject developing color print after exposure. Kodak and Polaroid instant films are not interchangeable; neither firm's cameras accept other firm's films. Courtesy Eastman Kodak Company.

Appendix

Metric Conversion Information

When Your Know	Multiply by	To Find
inches (in.)	25.4	millimetres (mm)
feet (ft.)	0.3048	metres (m)
miles (mi.)	1.609	kilometres (km)
ounces (oz.)	28.349	grams (g)
pounds (lbs.)	0.453	kilograms (kg)
pounds per square inch (psi.)	0.0703	kilograms per square centimetre (kg/sqcm)
cubic feet (cu. ft.)	0.0283	cubic meters
Fahrenheit temperature (F)	1.8 after subtracting 32	Celsius temperature (C)

ASA AND DIN FILM SPEEDS

ASA	DIN	ASA	DIN	ASA	DIN	ASA	DIN
6	9	25	15	100	21	400	27
8	10	32	16	125	22	500	28
10	11	40	17	160	23	640	29
12	12	50	18	200	24	800	30
16	13	64	19	250	25	1000	31
20	14	80	20	320	26	1250	32

Index